best ever garden plants

choosing the best plants for your garden

Susan Berry and Steve Bradley

HERMES HOUSE

This edition is published by Hermes House

Hermes House is an imprint of Anness Publishing Ltd
Hermes House, 88–89 Blackfriars Road, London SE1 8HA
tel. 020 7401 2077; fax 020 7633 9499; info@anness.com

A CIP catalogue record for this book is available from the British Library.

Publisher: Joanna Lorenz
Senior Editor: Caroline Davison
Designer: Ian Sandom
Production Controller: Mark Fennell
Plant Consultant: Tony Lord
Commissioned Photography: Sue Atkinson
Original Design: Patrick McLeavey & Partners

Previously published as part of a larger compendium, *Best Plants for Your Garden*

1 3 5 7 9 10 8 6 4 2

PAGE 1: *Lonicera* 'Etrusca'.
PAGE 2: *Polygonum* and *Iris*.
PAGE 3: *Philadelphus coronarius*.
PAGE 4: *Dianthus*.
PAGE 5: *Tradescantia virginiana*.

best ever
garden plants

CONTENTS

Introduction   6

PLANTS FOR DRY SUN   10

PLANTS FOR SHADE   24

PLANTS FOR ACID SOILS   36

PLANTS FOR ALKALINE SOILS   52

PLANTS FOR CLAY SOILS   68

MOISTURE-LOVING PLANTS   80

INDEX OF PLANTS   92
NOTES AND ACKNOWLEDGEMENTS   96

Introduction

A cottage-style border showing a blend of perennials and small shrubs including alliums, poppies, astrantia, elaeagnus, cistus and hostas.

For all gardeners, making the right selection of plants is the single most important ingredient for success in gardening. To do this, you need to be informed on several different levels: you need to be able to identify the overall look you are hoping to achieve and the kind of garden you want to create, and you also need to understand the conditions that determine which plants will grow successfully. One of the most important lessons for any novice gardener to grasp is that you cannot grow exactly what you want wherever you please.

Although you always want to try to manage nature, or at least influence it as much as you dare, the most successful gardeners are those who look at how plants grow in their natural habitat, and apply this to their own garden, working with nature wherever possible. The greater understanding you have of where plants grow best, and the more you understand their needs, the easier it becomes to grow them. The section on pages 7-8 explains these requirements in more detail.

PLANNING YOUR GARDEN

When planning a garden you must have some understanding of what your soil is like – whether it is acid or alkaline, heavy clay or light sand – and whether the climate is hot or cool, wet or dry. Immense strides have been made in plant breeding, and recent

innovations have allowed gardeners far greater freedom of choice than they had previously now that in many instances plants are bred to be both beautiful and tough. Even so, nature still plays by far the most important role, and a plant that naturally thrives in a damp or wet habitat will not flourish in hot dry sun as well. Its entire organism has evolved over thousands of years to cope with the particular conditions in which it originated, and usually it is only in similar conditions that it will continue to thrive.

Fortunately, some plants do withstand quite a wide range of climatic variations and are particularly well adapted, thriving surprisingly well in conditions very far removed from those of their natural habitat. The sensible gardener tries to pay attention to these needs, and to select his or her plants from within the range of those that are broadly suitable.

Whether planning an entire garden or just designing a border, you will probably want to include a range of different types to give height and variety to your plan. Try to remember that foliage is as important as flowers in the overall structure and shape of the garden, and make sure you pick a framework of plants with good shape or attractive foliage, on which the more ephemeral elements of the design such as perennials and annuals can be hung.

Flowers, while eye-catching, are not always the major element in the success of any garden design. It is also the way in which the garden is laid out and constructed: the organization of its hard surfaces including terraces and paths; any hedges and screens; the creation of a vertical element, in the form of climbing plants, shrubs and trees. These also give shelter and create pockets of dry shade which a further range of plants will enjoy. A selection of climbers and hedges is listed on page 9. Nature often tends to provide these variations unaided, but if they do not exist in your garden, you will have to make your own varied but viable micro-climate, thereby increasing the range you can grow, and also your own enjoyment.

Not many gardens have a naturally damp area which could support moisture-loving plants but a boggy patch or even a pond is easy to make and certainly gives you the opportunity to include these attractive plants.

Another important element when planning a garden is winter interest. Try to ensure you have a good number of evergreen shrubs or trees which will provide a structure for the garden during the winter months. Without them, the garden can look impossibly bleak and dull, when the foliage of most herbaceous perennials has disappeared, leaving you with bare stems and branches. In a new garden, ground cover can be an important element in the plan to help prevent the bare soil becoming engulfed in weeds. You can opt either for plants that naturally spread to cover the soil, or for those shrubs and perennials that have a spreading habit, thereby effectively suppressing weeds by their shady canopy. (See page 9 for a range of plants that are suitable for ground cover.)

CULTIVATION

Whatever plants you choose, you need to ensure that you look after them correctly. This means not only do you plant them where they are most likely to thrive, but you also attend to any special requirements, in terms of watering, feeding and pruning.

Most plants look far better when planted in largish groups rather than dotted about singly, and propagation is one of the easiest and cheapest ways to increase your stock of plants. When purchasing your plants initially, it is a good idea to pick plants that can be propagated easily and that are fairly fast to establish, so that building up your stock of plants and also furnishing the bare spaces in your garden are achieved relatively quickly.

Although many plants are more or less pest- and disease-free, others are singularly prone to various complaints and to attacks by a particular kind of insect. Hostas, for example, are notoriously easy prey to slugs, while tender young shoots, leaves and buds of many plants will quickly become infested with aphids in summer. You can do a lot to control these problems if you are forewarned when you select your plants. Hostas, for example, can be surrounded with a layer of grit, which deters slugs and snails, or, if you are not averse to chemical methods, you can use slug pellets. Particular problems for individual plants are indicated in each entry.

Like most humans, plants respond best to regular, systematic sensible care, and very rarely to the feast or famine principle of gardening. Try not to neglect your plants for a long period of time and then make up for it in one mammoth session of attention, whether it is feeding, watering, pruning or whatever. It is far better to keep a watchful eye on your plants, noting any problems as they arise, and nipping them in the bud, if you will forgive the expression, before they become more serious. Even the vexed problem of pruning is better if tackled after flowering on a week-by-week basis, rather than in one massive hit in late autumn or early spring.

HOW TO USE THIS BOOK

This book is divided into six sections which focus on some of the common conditions and basic needs of modern gardeners, with the idea that once you have identified these, you can then find some suitable plants for your purpose.

The plants we have selected in this book have been chosen on the basis of good overall performance: they are all reasonably easy to grow and have more than one good feature. Within the specific categories of need or condition identified, you will find a cross-section of the following types: trees, shrubs, herbaceous perennials, and climbers – the plants which usually make up the core planting of any garden, and occasional references to bulbs, tuberous plants and roses which many people like to grow. Annuals, which can be grown from seed in one season, and therefore are not a permanent feature in the garden, get only relatively minor coverage.

At the end of each section there is a cross reference list which itemises other plants that might be grown. Most plants will tolerate differing soil types and the chart on page 9 shows you which plants can be chosen if you need to consider more than one feature.

WHAT PLANTS NEED

Knowledge of what a plant requires in terms of light, water, temperature, soil type and nutrients is essential for good gardening. In addition, you also need to identify which of these requirements your garden can naturally provide, and how you can change the micro-environment within your garden if the conditions are not suitable for the plants you aspire (and in many instances perspire) to grow. For instance, in a dark situation, thinning existing plants will allow in more light, and in a damp garden, improving the soil drainage will encourage plants which prefer drier conditions. Alternatively, you may prefer to use your garden's natural dampness and enjoy the range of moisture-loving plants listed in chapter 6.

The plants you may wish to grow originate from many different areas of the world, where very different growing conditions exist. In their natural environment, some will grow in dense shade on the forest floor while others are exposed to intense bright sunlight for long periods of time. This wide diversity of natural habitat explains why the many different ornamental plants we grow require different conditions. The ability to adapt to unfamiliar conditions is a major reason for the popularity of many common plants. Of course, some plants are much more adaptable than others; classic examples are the forsythia, which seems to be flowering everywhere in the spring, and *Buddleja davidii*, which has been so successful at colonizing areas that many people now regard it as a weed.

Salvias, lilies, sambucus and daisies emphasized by the white of
Geranium clarkei *'Kashmir White' make a quiet corner in a mixed border.*

Plants pushing out onto gravel paths create a charming informality. Here Lavandula stoechas *and* Lychnis coronaria *catch the evening sun.*

LIGHT

Light is essential to all plants, as it provides the energy needed by the plant to manufacture food during daylight hours. Other activities within the plant are also influenced by light; for instance, the response to the hours of daylight within the 24-hour cycle will determine the time of year that flowers are produced. This response to the day-length is called photoperiodism, and explains why plants flower at specific times of the year, regardless of the prevailing weather conditions. As day-length appears to be a plant's main method of knowing which season is which, it is a factor which gardeners would love to be able to tamper with, but this can only realistically be done at great expense in a fully controlled environment, as in the production of pot plants such as poinsettias for Christmas. Even the most dedicated of gardeners does not have the time to do this.

The amount of light is also the main stimulus for autumn leaf fall in deciduous trees and shrubs, the trigger which starts this response being the shortening days of autumn. The various colour changes within the leaf are brought about by the chemical changes which occur when plant nutrients are drawn out of the leaf back into the stem. As a gardener you are able to influence (to some extent) the light intensity your plants receive by providing shade to reduce light levels. Alternatively, to raise light levels in a darkened corner, you could use mirrors and create light-reflective surfaces such as white gravel and paving. However, there is a selection of plants in chapter 2 that enjoys a shady situation, while plants that love sunny conditions are listed in chapter 1.

Generally speaking, most plants consist of roots, stems, leaves, flowers and usually fruits, many of which contain seeds. None of these parts functions in isolation. There is a close relationship between the individual parts of the plant and the plant's overall growth rate. Some plants are also scented and these are a particular favourite with gardeners.

THE SOIL

Although it is not easy to describe what soil actually is, we know that plants grow better when planted in the right type of soil. A basic understanding can help to create a good root environment for the plants you wish to grow. Soil is required by the gardener to have certain properties: the ability to hold moisture and air so that the plant's roots are not deprived of oxygen; the correct balance of nutrients; and the appropriate level of lime or acidity.

What makes growing plants more of a challenge is that many garden soils play host to a number of unwanted 'additives' such as weed seeds, stones (and occasionally builder's debris), pests and diseases. Heavy, clay soils are also difficult to work with and choosing plants that thrive in this situation is essential. Chapter 5 suggests a range of plants for clay soils.

Acidity and alkalinity are measured on a scale of pH which ranges from 0 to 14, with 0 being the most acid and 14 being the most alkaline. The influence of pH affects the solubility of minerals and hence their availability to plants. Acid conditions tend to encourage phosphorus deficiency and sometimes contain excess manganese and aluminium, while alkaline conditions can lead to a lack of manganese, boron, and phosphorus. Soil pH can also influence the number and type of beneficial soil-borne organisms, as well as the incidence of pests and diseases. For example, worms dislike a low pH, but leatherjackets and wireworms are more commonly found in acid conditions. What is the optimum pH? Again, the pH range for good plant growth varies depending upon the preference of the individual plants. Some plants are more sensitive than others and have quite specific requirements: lime-loving plants that prefer chalky (alkaline) soil are known as calcicoles, and lime-haters that like an acid soil are called calcifuges. These plants are listed in chapter 3 for acid soils and chapter 4 for chalky (alkaline) soils.

Many gardeners wish to grow the widest range of plants possible and the temptation is to try to manipulate the pH of the soil. Although this may be possible, to lower the soil pH is difficult, costly, and usually only a short-term measure, whereas raising soil pH is relatively easy and, if done correctly, can have beneficial effects on a long-term basis. If you really cannot resist the temptation to grow lime-hating plants and your soil has a pH reading of 6.0 or over, then by far the best option is to grow them in containers. That way you can exercise complete control over the pH of the compost (soil mix).

The question of what plants you can grow in your garden is now, therefore, a matter of turning to the appropriate section for your particular requirements.

Best Plants for a Variety of Conditions

The following selection of plants includes many of those featured in this book and represents the trees, shrubs, climbers and herbaceous perennials which have a range of useful features; they are, therefore, good all-rounders.

Plant	Acid soil	Alkaline soil	Clay soil	Moisture-loving	Shade	Dry/Sunny	Climbers/Hedges	Ground cover	Winter interest	Scent	Growth rate	Season of interest	Classification	Evergreen
Acanthus spinosus		◆	◆					◆			F	2	HP	
Acer palmatum	◆			◆					◆		S	3	T	
Actinidia kolomikta			◆			◆					M	2-3	C	
Agapanthus			◆			◆		◆			M	2-3	HP	
Amelanchier				◆					◆		S	1-3	S	
Arbutus	◆					◆	◆				M	134	T	
Aucuba		◆	◆		◆						M	2-3	S	•
Berberis						◆	◆	◆			M	2-3	S	●
Bergenia			◆					◆			S	1	HP	•
Buxus sempervirens							◆	◆	◆		S	1-4	S	•
Calluna	◆					◆	◆	◆			S	2-4	S	•
Camellia	◆				◆						S	12	S	•
Campsis			◆				◆	◆		◆	F	2-3	C	
Cercidiphyllum	◆					◆			◆	◆	M	3	T	
Cercis		◆	◆			◆				◆	M	123	S	
Crataegus		◆	◆			◆	◆				F	2-3	T	
Eccremocarpus		◆				◆	◆				F	2-3	C	•
Epimedium		◆		◆	◆		◆	◆			M	2-3	HP	•
Escallonia	◆	◆	◆			◆	◆				F	2-3	S	•
Festuca	◆				◆			◆	◆		M	1-4	HP	•
Ficus carica		◆				◆					S	2-3	S	
Filipendula		◆	◆	◆							M	2-3	HP	
Garrya		◆					◆	◆			M	1	S	•
Gaultheria	◆						◆	◆			S	234	S	•
Gleditsia	◆	◆				◆			◆		M	2-3	T	
Hamamelis	◆								◆	◆	M	1&3	S	
Hosta		◆	◆	◆				◆		◆	F	2-3	HP	
Ilex			◆			◆					S	2-4	T	•
Imperata	◆		◆	◆					◆	◆	M	3-4	HP	
Iris pseudacorus		◆	◆	◆							M	1-2	HP	
Kalmia latifolia	◆				◆						M	1-2	S	•
Laburnum	◆	◆				◆			◆		M	2-3	T	
Lathyrus	◆	◆				◆	◆			◆	F	2-3	CHP	
Lavandula		◆				◆		◆		◆	M	2	S	•
Lilium	◆				◆				◆	◆	F	1-2	HP	
Mahonia			◆		◆	◆		◆	◆	◆	M	3-4	S	•
Osmunda		◆	◆	◆					◆		M	3	HP	
Parrotia	◆							◆			S	1&3	T	
Parthenocissus			◆	◆			◆				F	2-3	C	
Pieris	◆				◆						M	1-2	S	•
Prunus		◆						◆			M	1&3	T	
Pyracantha	◆	◆			◆	◆	◆				M	2-3	S	
Rhus hirta		◆			◆	◆					M	3	S	
Rosa rugosa		◆				◆	◆			◆	F	2&3	S	
Rosmarinus		◆				◆		◆			M	2	S	•
Salvia officinalis	◆	◆				◆		◆			M	2-3	S	
Senecio 'Sunshine'		◆				◆		◆			M	2-3	S	
Stachys		◆				◆		◆			M	2	HP	
Stewartia	◆			◆	◆				◆		M	2	S	
Taxus		◆			◆						M	3-4	T	•
Viburnum		◆	◆			◆	◆	◆	◆	◆	M	341	S	●
Vitis		◆	◆			◆	◆				F	3-4	C	
Wisteria		◆	◆			◆	◆			◆	F	2-3	C	
Zenobia	◆				◆						S	2-3	S	

KEY

Growth rate
S – Slow
M – Medium
F – Fast

Season of interest
1 – Spring
2 – Summer
3 – Autumn
4 – Winter

Classification
T – Tree
S – Shrub
HP – Herbaceous Perennial
C – Climber
CHP – Climbing Hardy Perennial

Evergreen
• – Some varieties are evergreen

PLANTS *for* DRY SUN

For sunny, dry areas in your garden, plants from the hotter areas of the world are a good choice because they thrive in these conditions. Many are distinguished by divided, waxy or felted leaves. Grey-leaved plants, such as lavender and senecio, are typical examples.

ABOVE: Convolvulus cneorum, *a grey-leaved sub-shrub, thrives in hot dry conditions and produces a profusion of delicate white flowers.*

OPPOSITE: *A garden in summer with the climbing roses just coming into bloom. The roses give additional height to the border and the mixed colours of the herbaceous perennials provide a splendid contrast.*

ABOVE: *A mixed border, with the front edge in sun, provides a home for a cottage-garden style planting of opium poppies in the front, contrasting with the silvery-grey Miss Willmott's Ghost* (Eryngium giganteum) *and the spires of the purple form of the burning bush* (Dictamnus albus *var.* purpureus) *behind.*

Anyone who has travelled abroad to the Mediterranean, California or Australia, especially in the spring, will realize that a hot and dry site is by no means a problem in a garden. If you select your plants carefully, you can create a fine display which will provide colour and interest. Start with some of the best known plants from the Mediterranean: lavender, rosemary, sage, salvia and santolina, rock roses (cistus), helichrysum (the everlasting flower) and marigolds. These are just some of the plants that like a position in full sun and dry soil.

The plants which survive these conditions tend to have evolved and adapted in order to cope with high temperatures and low rainfall. These adaptations are often what make the plants so attractive. *Convolvulus cneorum*, with its silver and grey foliage, appears this colour because it has developed a coating of fine hairs on the leaf surface, which has the effect of reducing moisture loss and reflecting sunlight. Other plants, such as *Senecio* 'Sunshine' (now properly called *Brachyglottis*), have modified their leaves by thickening them to protect the inside, while the underside of the leaf remains felted. Brooms, such as *Genista aetnensis*, reduce moisture loss by having hardly any leaves at all, but thin tough stems.

The soil in which these plants grow in the wild is often poor and impoverished. It may be almost pure sand or gravel, which makes it very quick to drain, and in summer there is very little natural moisture. There is little organic matter too, as any fallen leaves burn up quickly, or there may be just a very shallow scraping of soil over solid rock, the roots clinging on for life by penetrating cracks and crevices.

In the garden, these conditions can exist naturally or can be created artificially; where the garden is of thin shallow soil overlying solid rock, for example, or where the subsoil is pure sand or gravel which has found its way to the surface, as can happen in a new garden if the topsoil has been removed during building works. Perhaps you have a south-facing border against a house wall, particularly if there is a path or patio to the other side, or a south-facing, sloping garden; these also tend towards dryness, and more so if the soil is also sandy.

The main problem with such soils is lack of moisture for the plants. Improving the soil is difficult, as any organic matter you try to incorporate is quickly burnt up, and the plant nutrients you do apply will be washed through the soil along with the water. On the positive side, however, dry soils are quick to warm up in spring, and if you can achieve a cover of plants that like this environment, they will soon start to help themselves by using their natural adaptations to conserve moisture.

RIGHT: *The brilliant white flowers of* Anthemis punctata *ssp.* cupaniana *with their yellow eyes make it an ideal subject to plant at the edge of a gravel garden.*

BELOW: *A gravel garden provides a home for alpines that enjoy both sun and free draining soil: here the yellow flowers of the helianthemum and the pink spreading saponaria, tumbling Ted, provide a foil for the French lavender.*

Acantholimon glumaceum

Prickly thrift
HEIGHT: 6in (15cm) • Hardy
FLOWERING SEASON: Summer

An evergreen perennial with a low, cushion-forming habit; the stems often root into the soil as the plant spreads across the ground. The flowers are produced in small, short spikes of up to eight star-shaped, pink blooms which are carried above the spiny, spear-shaped, bluish-green leaves, and arranged in tight rosettes on the stems. Propagation is by softwood cuttings taken from non-flowering shoots in spring and summer and rooted in a cold frame.

Aethionema 'Warley Ruber'

Persian candytuft
HEIGHT: 6in (15cm) • Hardy
FLOWERING SEASON: Spring/summer

This colourful evergreen sub-shrub has tiny strap-like leaves which are a bluish-green colour. It has a naturally spreading habit and forms a dense mat of foliage over the soil. The small cross-shaped flowers are a deep rose-pink and grow in loose clusters on the tips of the shoots. Often grown in the rock garden, this plant needs an open, free-draining soil to grow well. Trim the plants in mid-summer after the flowers are over and propagate by taking softwood cuttings from the new growth, either in the late summer, or in the spring.

Agapanthus Headbourne Hybrids

African lily
HEIGHT: 3ft (1m) • Moderately hardy
FLOWERING SEASON: Mid/late summer

A clump-forming herbaceous perennial with deep green strap-like leaves up to 2½ft (75cm) long and large clusters of deep blue flowers produced from July onwards. Cultivars, such as Headbourne Hybrids, are usually hardier than many of the species. They like full sun, and have thick fleshy roots which provide a good water store and drought tolerance. In northern areas they require winter protection. Propagate by division in spring.

Anthemis punctata ssp. *cupaniana*

Chamomile/Dog fennel
HEIGHT: 12in (30cm) • Hardy
FLOWERING SEASON: Early summer

An evergreen herbaceous perennial that is invaluable for a dry sunny garden. It forms a loose cushion of finely cut, silvery-grey, aromatic foliage, which turns green in winter. The white daisy-like flowers have a golden centre, or 'eye', and are carried singly above the leaves on short erect stems. No regular pruning is required but the dead flower heads are usually removed in autumn. Propagation is by semi-ripe basal cuttings taken in summer.

Aster novi-belgii 'Jenny'

Michaelmas daisy
HEIGHT: 2½ft (75cm) • Hardy
FLOWERING SEASON: Early autumn

This popular herbaceous perennial has mid to deep green leaves carried on sturdy erect green stems, they are roughly elliptical but terminate in a sharp point. The colourful daisy-like flowers are produced in large quantities in autumn. Many reliable named cultivars are available: *A. n-b.* 'Royal Ruby' has deep red flowers, and 'White Ladies' has white flowers and dark foliage. They flourish in sun or part shade and are generally soil tolerant. Propagate by softwood cuttings in summer, or division in early spring.

Buddleja alternifolia

Butterfly bush
HEIGHT: 15ft (4.5m) • Hardy
FLOWERING SEASON: Summer

A large deciduous shrub with graceful arching stems covered in grey-green, narrow strap-like leaves, which have a bluish underside. Clusters of small, delicately fragrant, lilac-blue flowers are produced in early summer on the previous year's wood. Prune after flowering but if left unpruned the shrub develops into a sprawling plant with a semi-weeping habit. An interesting cultivar, *B. a.* 'Argentea', has hairy silver-grey leaves. This plant is easy to propagate by softwood cuttings in summer or hardwood cuttings in winter.

Campanula persicifolia

Peach-leaved bellflower
HEIGHT: 3ft (1m) • Hardy
FLOWERING SEASON: Mid-late summer

This clump-forming, evergreen, herbaceous perennial has long, narrow, mid green, leathery leaves which grow in tight rosettes. The bell-shaped flowers are produced close to the main stem, and range in colour from bluish-purple to pure white. Cultivars include 'Telham Beauty', which has deep blue flowers, and *C. p.* var. *planiflora* f. *alba,* which has pure white ones. Propagate by seed sown in early and mid-spring, cuttings taken in mid- and late spring, or dividing the plants in mid-autumn.

Catalpa bignonioides

Indian bean tree
HEIGHT: 50ft (15m) • Hardy
FLOWERING SEASON: Summer

This outstanding deciduous tree has an open, spreading habit and, in mature specimens, a deeply grooved bark. It is valued for its tolerance of urban pollution. The large, heart-shaped leaves are tinged with purple as they open, turning light-green as they mature. In summer white, bell-shaped flowers with yellow and purple markings are produced, followed by long hanging pods which stay throughout winter. There is a striking golden-leaved cultivar: *C. b.* 'Aurea'. Propagate in summer using softwood tip cuttings.

Catananche caerulea

Cupid's dart/Blue cupidone
HEIGHT: 2ft (60cm) • Hardy
FLOWERING SEASON: Summer

This clump forming perennial known as cupid's dart, has narrow, grey-green, strap-like leaves carried on tall erect mid green stems and masses of daisy-like, purple-blue flowers throughout the summer. They like a sunny, open position and light, well-drained soil. There are a number of named cultivars: *C. c.* 'Major', has lavender blue flowers, *C. c.* 'Perry's White', is the most popular white cultivar. Named cultivars must be propagated by root cuttings taken in winter.

Clarkia elegans

Clarkia
HEIGHT: 2ft (60cm) • Hardy
FLOWERING SEASON: Late summer/autumn

This popular annual is grown for its colourful display of summer flowers, the leaves are narrow, oval and mid green in colour. The flowers are produced in bold spikes on erect green stems in colours which range through white, salmon, orange, purple, scarlet and lavender. In addition, double-flowered forms are also available; *C. e.* Love Affair, is a mixed colour strain with large double flowers and compact growth. Propagation is by seed sown outdoors in early spring. Thin the seedlings to 9-12in (20-30cm) apart.

Convolvulus cneorum

HEIGHT: 2½ft (75cm) • Moderately hardy
FLOWERING SEASON: Late spring/early autumn

A rather surprising member of the same genus as the pernicious bindweed, this is a slightly tender evergreen shrub of compact and low-growing bushy habit, with silvery, silky, narrow pointed leaves, on silver hairy stems. The short-lived flowers, produced at the tips of the shoots from late spring to early autumn, are a soft pink in tight bud, opening to pure white with a small golden-yellow eye in the centre. It prefers a sheltered position in well-drained but nutrient-poor soil in full sun. Propagation is by semi-ripe cuttings, taken in mid-summer.

Cortaderia selloana 'Aureolineata'

Pampas grass
HEIGHT: 8ft (2.5m) • Moderately hardy
FLOWERING SEASON: Summer/autumn

A bold, showy, clump-forming ornamental grass, with narrow, pale to mid green, spear-shaped, evergreen leaves, which have razor sharp edges. The flowers, which are carried in majestic silvery-white plumes tinged red or purple in autumn, are held high above the arching leaves on erect almost white stems. A popular cultivar is *C. s.* 'Sunningdale Silver', which has long-lasting, large, silver flower-plumes. Propagation is by division in spring; select female plants for a better flower display.

Corylus avellana 'Contorta'

Cobnut/Hazelnut
HEIGHT: 10ft (3m) • Hardy
FLOWERING SEASON: Early spring

This large deciduous shrub is grown for its curiously twisted branches and twigs. The broadly oval, mid green leaves have a noticeably toothed margin and turn a deep gold in autumn. The female flowers are very small, but the long yellow male catkins are very attractive in late winter. It likes well-drained limy soil and mortar rubble may be added before planting if the soil is lime-deficient. It is best to propagate by layering one-year-old shoots, but rooting will take up to a year.

Crataegus laciniata

Hawthorn
HEIGHT: 22ft (7m) • Hardy
FLOWERING SEASON: Spring

A beautiful small ornamental tree, with sparsely thorned, lax branches covered in felt when young. The deeply cut, downy leaves are dark green above and grey-green beneath. The large fruits are a pinkish-yellow later turning red and hang on the tree most of the winter. Propagation is by budding in summer or grafting in early spring. The bacterial disease fireblight causes withering and progressive die-back of young shoots.

Cytisus battandieri

Pineapple broom/Moroccan broom
HEIGHT: 12ft (4m) • Moderately hardy
FLOWERING SEASON: Early summer

A spectacular semi-evergreen open shrub best grown against the shelter of a west- or south-facing wall, the pineapple bush carries large racemes of the pineapple-scented flowers which give it its name from early to midsummer. Like all brooms it prefers light well-drained soil but it can be grown successfully on heavier land provided plenty of sand and leaf mould are worked into the ground before planting. Propagate by semi-ripe cuttings taken in late summer.

Cytisus × kewensis

Broom
HEIGHT: 2ft (60cm) • Hardy
FLOWERING SEASON: Late spring

This low-growing shrub was raised at Kew Gardens, in England in 1891 and has been popular ever since. In spring, cascades of creamy-yellow, sweet-pea-shaped blooms cover the bush, obscuring the stems and leaves. The mid green leaves are small, strap-like, covered in fine hairs and grow sparsely along the lax, twiggy, green stems. This plant should be pruned after flowering but it does not respond well to hard pruning or being moved. Propagation is by semi-ripe cuttings with a heel taken in summer.

Davidia involucrata

Dove tree/Handkerchief tree
HEIGHT: 50ft (15m) • Hardy
FLOWERING SEASON: Late spring

This beautiful tree is grown for the striking display of large, white, modified leaf bracts, from which it gets its common name 'handkerchief tree'. The insignificant flowers appear in small clusters on mature plants in late spring. The mid green, heart-shaped leaves have dense hairs on the underside, and in autumn turn a bright golden-yellow with a red tinge at the margin. It likes a sunny position and deep well-drained soil. Propagation is by seed sown in autumn or semi-ripe cuttings taken in early summer.

Diascia fetcaniensis

HEIGHT: 12in (30cm) • Half-hardy
FLOWERING SEASON: Summer

These plants are slender, low-growing annuals or short-lived perennials with dark green, glossy, broadly oval leaves, with a toothed margin. The tube-shaped, rosy-pink, lilac or apricot flowers open out into a shell-like bloom with spotted throat. They are produced in large flushes on the tips of slender green shoots. A popular cultivar, *D.* 'Ruby Field', has salmon-pink flowers. They like sun and rich, moist, well-drained soil that does not dry out. Propagate by cuttings taken in late summer. (This plant is often mistakenly identified as nemesia.)

Dorotheanthus bellidiformis

Livingstone daisy/Ice plant/Fig marigold
HEIGHT: 4in (10cm) • Tender
FLOWERING SEASON: Summer/autumn

Some mesembryanthemums have become dorotheanthus, but this is still the Livingstone daisy, which is well adapted to surviving in dry, arid conditions. Low and spreading in habit, its narrow, light green, tube-like leaves have a glistening appearance. In a dry sunny position it produces brightly coloured, small, daisy-like flowers. The colour range includes white, pink, carmine, salmon, apricot and orange. Propagate by sowing seeds indoors in early spring.

Echinops bannaticus 'Taplow Blue'

Globe thistle
HEIGHT: 4ft (1.2m) • Hardy
FLOWERING SEASON: Late summer

An attractive upright perennial with narrow leaves and palish-blue thistle-like heads carried on branching stems in late summer. Globe thistles flourish in ordinary garden soil and like a sunny position. They are useful plants for the herbaceous border as their pale, neutral colour provides a good foil for brighter plants. Propagate by division in the autumn or by root cuttings taken in mild weather in winter.

Eryngium bourgatii

Sea holly
HEIGHT: 2½ft (75cm) • Hardy
FLOWERING SEASON: Summer/autumn

At first glance, these tough herbaceous perennials look like a cross between a holly and a thistle, but they are not related to either. The tough, spiny, coarsely toothed leaves vary in colour from dark green to silvery-blue. The flowers, which often look very like teasel heads, are metallic silvery-blue, darkening with age, with a collar of broad spines at the base; they are held on strong wiry stems above the leaves. Propagation is by division or root cuttings in spring.

Escallonia 'Slieve Donard'

Escallonia
HEIGHT: 14ft (4.5m) • Not fully hardy
FLOWERING SEASON: Late spring/early summer

Escallonias are handsome evergreen shrubs which can be grown either as hedges, in the shrubbery, or against a wall. They have an attractive range of flower colours from white through pink to scarlet. The small, bell-shaped flowers are produced in clusters on short spur-like branches above the glossy oval leaves, dark green above and pale green beneath. They like sun and well-drained soil and are an excellent plant for southern coastal regions. Propagates very easily from softwood cuttings taken in midsummer.

Eucalyptus gunnii

Cider gum
HEIGHT: 35ft (10.5m) • Moderately hardy
FLOWERING SEASON: Autumn/winter

The cider gum is an evergreen tree that comes from Australia and is grown mainly for its blue-grey, leathery-textured leaves and stems. The leaf shape varies with the age of the plant: the juvenile leaves are almost circular and appear to clasp the short stems on which they are produced, but as the plant matures the new leaves are strap-like and hang down vertically. Young trees have a blue-grey bark. Eucalyptus can be cut to the ground each spring and grown as shrubs. Propagation is by seed sown in spring.

Galtonia candicans

Summer hyacinth
HEIGHT: 4ft (1.2m) • Moderately hardy
FLOWERING SEASON: Late summer/early autumn

These outstanding late-flowering bulbs have leaves which are a bluish grey-green, widely strap-shaped and quite thick and fleshy. Single stems carry a head of large, slightly scented, drooping, white bells, with pale green markings at the base of each petal. These bulbs make an attractive display at a time when many other plants are looking jaded. They like a sheltered sunny site. They produce seed very freely and may become invasive. Propagation is by seed sown in spring or bulblets in autumn.

Genista aetnensis

Mount Etna broom
HEIGHT: 25ft (8m) • Hardy
FLOWERING SEASON: Summer

This is a large elegant shrub, with many slender drooping, bright green branches, which are practically leafless. The tough, sparse leaves are mid green and strap-like, with fine, white, silky hairs. The golden-yellow, heavily scented, pea-like flowers are produced in large quantities at the tips of the shoots in midsummer. It likes full sun and will tolerate almost any soil conditions except waterlogging. Propagation is by seed sown in spring.

Gleditsia triacanthos 'Sunburst'

Honey locust
HEIGHT: 30ft (9m) • Moderately hardy
FLOWERING SEASON: Midsummer

A beautiful small tree ideal for giving light shade in the garden, provided the site is not exposed. The small, delicate leaflets are arranged in large numbers (up to 32) along a tough green leaf stalk, although a glossy mid green, the most popular cultivar is the golden-leaved *G. t.* 'Sunburst', and there is a purple-leaved cultivar, *G. t.* 'Rubylace'. Propagation is by seed sown under protection in spring or the named cultivars are increased by grafting in early spring.

Gypsophila repens 'Rosa Schönheit'

Chalk plant
HEIGHT: 3ft (1m) • Hardy
FLOWERING SEASON: Summer

These cottage garden favourites have thin, strap-like grey-green leaves very similar to those of the carnation, carried on thick, grey-green stems. Masses of very small, usually white, flowers are produced in large clusters. There are dwarf and pink-flowered forms. *G. repens* 'Rosea' is low-growing, 4-6in (10-15cm), and spreads to form a dense mat, with rose-pink flowers. Propagate by root cuttings taken when dormant.

× Halimiocistus wintonensis

HEIGHT: 2ft (60cm) • Not fully hardy
FLOWERING SEASON: Summer

This hybrid evergreen plant makes a low, spreading bush with small tough, slightly hairy, grey-green leaves supported on thin, grey-green, semi-prostrate stems. The small, saucer-shaped flowers are white with a red blotch at the base of each petal and a yellow centre to the bloom. The flowers open early in the morning and die the same day, leaving a carpet of petals around the plant. It likes full sun and fertile well-drained soil but will require shelter if grown in colder areas. Propagation is by small semi-ripe cuttings taken in summer.

Helianthemum 'Amy Baring'

Rock rose/Sun rose
HEIGHT: 3-4in (7.5-10cm) • Hardy
FLOWERING SEASON: Late summer/autumn

A dwarf and very drought-resistant evergreen shrub with small, oval, pale green leaves covered in fine hairs. The small, saucer-shaped flowers are produced in massed flushes, close to the ground on short stems. Good cultivars are *H.* 'Rhodanthe Carneum' with pink flowers and grey foliage, 'Wisley Primrose', soft golden-yellow flowers, and 'Wisley White', pure white flowers and grey foliage. Cut back lightly after flowering. Propagate by semi-ripe heel cuttings taken in late summer.

Helichrysum italicum

Curry plant
HEIGHT: 15in (35cm) • Moderately hardy
FLOWERING SEASON: Summer

This dwarf shrub has a dense, bushy habit and short, narrow silvery-grey, aromatic leaves which smell of curry when they are crushed or when the weather is very hot and sunny. The flowers grow in broad clusters of small, oblong, mustard-yellow flower-heads on long upright white shoots. It likes sun and well-drained soil. If not pruned with shears immediately after flowering, this shrub will spread, leaving an open, bare centre. Propagation is by semi-ripe cuttings taken with a heel in summer.

Hibiscus syriacus 'Oiseau Bleu'

Hibiscus
HEIGHT: 10ft (3m) • Moderately hardy
FLOWERING SEASON: Late summer

A large upright deciduous shrub with deeply notched dark green leaves. *H. s.* 'Oiseau Blue' carries large lilac-blue flowers with a red centre from late summer to mid autumn. Hibiscus come from the mallow family, *Malvaceae,* and vary from hardy to frost tender. They like full sun and rich well-drained soil. Among the best garden plants are the species, *H. syriacus* which is white with a red centre, and its cultivar *H. s.* 'Woodbridge' which is deep pink with a dark red centre.

Hibiscus syriacus 'Red Heart'

Hibiscus
Height: 10ft (3m) • Moderately hardy
FLOWERING SEASON: Late summer

Another popular cultivar of *H. syriacus,* 'Red Heart' has large white flowers with conspicuous red centres. Hibiscus should be planted in early spring or late autumn as background plants in a herbaceous border in the milder parts of the country. Little pruning is required but they can be thinned out in spring if the shrub is becoming over-crowded. Propagated by semi-ripe cuttings taken in summer and inserted in sandy soil in a cold frame.

Hypericum 'Hidcote'

St John's wort
HEIGHT: 4ft (1.2m) • Hardy
FLOWERING SEASON: Late summer/early autumn

This is a deciduous to semi-evergreen shrub with a dense bushy habit and thin, grey-green stems which turn pale-brown as they age. The small strap-like leaves are deep green on the upper surface with a slight blue-green sheen on the underside. The golden yellow saucer-shaped flowers are produced in clusters from late summer to early autumn. *H.* 'Hidcote Variegated' has a white margin to the leaf. Propagation is by semi-ripe cuttings taken with a heel in summer and autumn.

Ilex aquifolium 'Silver Queen'

Holly
HEIGHT: 15ft (4.5m) • Hardy
FLOWERING SEASON: Spring/summer

The hollies, the evergreen shrubs associated with Christmas, all have small, white, star-shaped flowers, with red, orange, yellow or even white berries produced on the female plants in winter. The leaves vary in colour but have sharp spines around the margin. Popular cultivars are *I. aquifolium* 'Silver Queen' with dark green leaves and a silver margin and *I. × altaclerensis* 'Golden King', with a golden margin. All of them prefer well-drained soil. Propagation is by semi-ripe cuttings taken in summer.

Kniphofia 'Royal Standard'

Red-hot poker/Torch lily
HEIGHT: 3ft (1m) • Moderately hardy
FLOWERING SEASON: Late summer

A familiar sight in many borders in late summer red-hot pokers carry their spears of red-tipped buds opening to yellow flowers above grass-like tufts of leaves. They prefer full sun and fertile well-drained soil and they do not do well in soil that becomes water-logged. The crowns may need protection in winter in hard weather. *K.* 'Little Maid' carries pale creamy-yellow, whitish flowers and *K.* 'Samuel's Sensation' deep orange ones. The plants resent being disturbed. Propagate by division in spring.

Laburnum × watereri 'Vossii'

Voss's laburnum
HEIGHT: 28ft (9m) • Hardy
FLOWERING SEASON: Late spring

A well-known flowering tree which produces large quantities of long, trailing clusters (racemes) of deep golden-yellow, pea-like flowers in late spring. In autumn the small, grey-brown pods split open to release small black seeds, which are poisonous. The grey-green leaves, which have a glossy upper surface and paler underside, are made up of three small leaflets. Laburnums grow in any but waterlogged soil but have a brittle root system and must be permanently staked. Propagate by grafting in spring.

Lavandula angustifolia

Lavender
HEIGHT: 3ft (1m) • Hardy
FLOWERING SEASON: Mid/late summer

This evergreen perennial has long, narrow, aromatic, silver-grey leaves covered with fine, felt-like hairs which are very effective in reducing moisture loss. The small, tube-like flowers are carried in narrow clusters, on tough, square stems. The most commonly grown cultivar, *L. a.* 'Hidcote', has strongly scented, deep purple-blue flowers and a compact bushy habit. *L. a.* 'Alba' is white and *L. a.* 'Rosea', pink. Propagation is by semi-ripe cuttings with a heel in summer.

Liriope muscari

Lilyturf
HEIGHT: 18in (45cm) • Hardy
FLOWERING SEASON: Late summer/late autumn

This clump-forming perennial has glossy, deep green, grass-like leaves. A network of rhizomes below ground provides a spreading habit which makes it ideal for ground cover. The thick clusters of flower spikes bear violet-blue, bell-shaped flowers.
L. m. 'Curly Twist' has lilac flowers flushed with burgundy and spirally twisting leaves.
L. m. 'Variegata' has a bold yellow stripe along the leaf margin. Propagation is by division in early spring.

Lithodora diffusa 'Heavenly Blue'

Gromwell
HEIGHT: 4in (10cm) • Hardy • pH
FLOWERING SEASON: Summer/late autumn

This prostrate, spreading plant is perfect for a hot, dry position, the slender stems are covered with small, dull green leaves which are spear-shaped and covered with fine hairs to reduce moisture loss. Small, deep-blue, funnel-shaped flowers are produced in vast quantities from early summer onwards. Hard pruning in spring will prevent the plant becoming straggly. Propagation is by semi-ripe cuttings taken in midsummer.

Lychnis chalcedonica

Jerusalem cross/Maltese cross
HEIGHT: 3ft (1m) • Hardy
FLOWERING SEASON: Summer

A neat clump-forming perennial which bears large clustered heads of flowers of an intense pure scarlet colour in early summer. It is easily grown and does best in full sun in fertile well-drained soil but it prefers soil which does not dry out. The cultivar *L. c.* 'Alba' is white. Other species include *L. flos-cuculi*, the ragged robin or cuckoo flower, which grows wild in Europe and Great Britain, its rose-pink flowers are extremely showy. Propagate by division of the roots in early spring.

Macleaya microcarpa

Plume poppy
HEIGHT: 6ft (1.8m) • Hardy
FLOWERING SEASON: Summer

Known as the plume poppy, this is an invasive herbaceous perennial which is particulary useful for the back of the border or for areas of woodland garden, since it does well in dappled shade as well as sun. The leaves are handsome, grey-green in colour, large and deeply lobed, the individually insignificant flowers are carried in tall plumes, in a soft bronze-pink shade. It grows in any soil but prefers soil that is well-manured and does not dry out. Divide and replant in autumn.

Nepeta × faassenii

Catmint
HEIGHT: 18in (45cm) • Hardy
FLOWERING SEASON: Late spring/autumn

This low-growing, bushy perennial is used for ground cover or as an edging plant for borders. The mounds of narrowly oval, grey-green leaves are arranged on short, square, grey stems, the tips terminating in tubular lavender-blue, salvia-like flowers which are held above the foliage. The cultivar *N.* 'Six Hills Giant', which is generally grown, is larger, with flower spikes up to 3ft (1m) high. It prefers a light soil and sunny position. Propagate by division in winter or by stem cutting in spring.

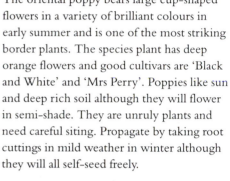

Oenothera missouriensis

Evening primrose
HEIGHT: 8in (20cm) • Hardy
FLOWERING SEASON: Mid/late summer

An excellent perennial for a hot, sunny spot. The spear-shaped, mid green leaves are carried on reddish-green, prostrate stems with upward-turning growing tips. The large, golden-yellow, bell-shaped flowers which open in the evening are produced continuously from early to late summer. It prefers a well-drained soil in sun or light shade. Cut down to ground level in autumn. Propagation is by seed sown in spring or by division in late winter.

Osteospermum 'Buttermilk'

HEIGHT: 2ft (60cm) • Half hardy
FLOWERING SEASON: Summer/autumn

Evergreen semi-woody perennials which will require protection in cold areas, osteospermums flower continually from midsummer through to the autumn carrying their daisy-like flowers on single stems above narrow deep green foliage. The most popular cultivars are 'Buttermilk', 'Cannington Roy', pink with dark eyes, 'Silver Sparkler', 'Tresco Purple', deep purple-red, and 'Whirligig', bluish-white with flower heads that look like the spokes of a wheel with drops on the end. They prefer sun and well-drained soil. Propagate by cuttings of non-flowering shoots in midsummer.

Papaver orientale 'Mrs Perry'

Oriental poppy
HEIGHT: 3ft (1m) • Hardy
FLOWERING SEASON: Summer

The oriental poppy bears large cup-shaped flowers in a variety of brilliant colours in early summer and is one of the most striking border plants. The species plant has deep orange flowers and good cultivars are 'Black and White' and 'Mrs Perry'. Poppies like sun and deep rich soil although they will flower in semi-shade. They are unruly plants and need careful siting. Propagate by taking root cuttings in mild weather in winter although they will all self-seed freely.

Parrotia persica

Persian ironwood
HEIGHT: 15ft (4.5m) • Hardy
FLOWERING SEASON: Late winter/early spring

A small deciduous tree with a wide-spreading habit and attractive autumn leaf colours. The leaves, which are roughly oval with a rounded base, are mid green until turning crimson-red and gold in the autumn. Small crimson flowers appear before the leaves, and the bark of mature plants flakes off in patches to reveal interesting patterns in the winter. The flowers may be killed by late frosts. There is also a weeping cultivar, *P. p.* 'Pendula'. Propagation is by softwood cuttings taken in summer or by seed sown in autumn.

Penstemon 'Apple Blossom'

Beard tongue
HEIGHT: 18in (45cm) • Moderately hardy
FLOWERING SEASON: Midsummer

A large genus of annuals, perennials, sub-shrubs and shrubs, the most popular are the semi-evergreen perennials which carry sprays of flowers above narrow green foliage throughout the summer. Among the best known cultivars are 'Alice Hindley', 'Apple Blossom' and 'Andenken an Friedrich Hahn' syn. 'Garnet'. They must have a sunny position in rich well-drained soil and will not flourish in poor conditions. Propagate by taking semi-ripe cuttings in summer or division in spring.

Perovskia atriplicifolia

Azure sage/Russian sage
HEIGHT: 4ft (1.2m) • Hardy
FLOWERING SEASON: Late summer/mid autumn

This deciduous shrub has thin grey-white stems which carry the narrowly oval, coarsely toothed, grey-green, aromatic foliage. The violet-blue, salvia-like flowers are produced in long slender spikes at the tips of the shoots. The best-known hybrid is *P.* 'Blue Spire', which has larger blue flowers and deeply cut grey-green leaves. Average winter frosts will cut the plant down to the ground, but it grows up again from the base in spring. Propagation is by softwood cuttings taken in late spring.

Ruta graveolens 'Jackman's Blue'

Rue
HEIGHT: 4ft (1.2m) • Hardy
FLOWERING SEASON: Summer/autumn

This is a bushy sub-shrub with leaves which are blue-green, oval and deeply divided to give a fern-like appearance with small, mustard-yellow flowers on the tip of each shoot. *R. g.* 'Jackman's Blue' has a more compact habit and brighter, blue-grey foliage. *R. g.* 'Variegata' has creamy-white and green variegated leaves. Propagation is by semi-ripe cuttings taken in late summer. This plant has sap which is a skin irritant.

Salvia officinalis Purpurascens Group

Sage
HEIGHT: 4ft (1.2m) • Hardy perennial
FLOWERING SEASON: Late summer/autumn

The true sage has dull green leaves with a roughly textured surface, arranged in pairs on erect, square stems, often with a reddish tinge. The tubular flowers open into a funnel shape, and are produced in clusters at the tips of the stems or from the leaf joints. The Purpurascens Group have purple leaves and *S. o.* 'Icterina' variegated yellow ones. Propagation is by semi-ripe cuttings taken in late spring or late summer.

Senecio 'Sunshine'

Daisy bush
HEIGHT: 3ft (1m) • Hardy
FLOWERING SEASON: Summer

The correct name for this shrub is now *Brachyglottis* Dunedin Hybrids Group 'Sunshine'. It forms a dense, broad-based mound and the leaves are silvery-grey at first, turning grey-green on the upper surface as they age. Sprays of silvery buds open to reveal yellow daisy-like flowers which are arranged in broad flat clusters. Prune after flowering to prevent the plant becoming straggly. Propagation is by semi-ripe cuttings taken with a heel in summer.

Sophora tetraptera

New Zealand laburnum
HEIGHT: 10ft (3m) • Not fully hardy
FLOWERING SEASON: Late spring

This large evergreen shrub or small tree will only grow well in a sheltered location. The foliage consists of rows of small, oblong, light green leaves which are held together by a tough, greenish-brown leafstalk. In spring a profusion of small, yellow, tubular flowers are produced in pendant clusters on the shoot tips, followed by winged fruits containing the seeds. The cultivar *S. microphylla* 'Early Gold' has pale yellow flowers and fern-like foliage. Propagation is by semi-ripe cuttings taken in early summer.

Spartium junceum

Spanish broom
HEIGHT: 10ft (3m) • Hardy
FLOWERING SEASON: Summer/early autumn

This deciduous flowering shrub has thin, tubular straggling branches which have a weeping appearance, the green stems make the plant seem evergreen. The small, inconspicuous leaves are short-lived, oval, mid green and covered in fine hairs. The large, pea-like flowers are bright golden-yellow and fragrant, they are carried at the tips of the new growth. It likes fairly poor soil and should be trimmed in early spring but does not respond well to hard pruning into old wood. Propagation is by seed sown in spring.

Stachys byzantina

Rabbit's ears/Lamb's tongue
HEIGHT: 16in (40cm) • Hardy
FLOWERING SEASON: Summer

This low growing, evergreen perennial is one of the most attractive and useful ground-cover plants for light soil and a hot sunny position. Its furry leaves which are covered in silvery hairs, give the plant a silver, grey or blue appearance, according to the light. The small, mauve flowers appear on white fluffy spikes up to about 16in (40cm) high. The cultivar *S. b.* 'Silver Carpet' is excellent ground cover. Propagation is by division in spring, although in summer it may be possible to find stems that have already rooted.

Tamarix ramosissima

Tamarisk
HEIGHT: 15ft (4.5m) • Hardy
FLOWERING SEASON: Late summer

An excellent plant for hot exposed sites, or coastal regions because it tolerates salt spray. The slender, gracefully arching, reddish-brown branches carry plumes of narrow, conifer-like foliage. The pink flowers are produced on long thin spikes during the summer. There are cultivars with darker flowers: the rose-pink, *T. r.* 'Rosea', the pale red *T. r.* 'Rubra'. Propagation is by semi-ripe cuttings taken with a heel in summer or hardwood cuttings in winter.

Yucca filamentosa

Adam's needle
HEIGHT: 2-3ft (60-90cm) • Moderately hardy
FLOWERING SEASON: Late summer

A striking evergreen shrub, generally grown as an architectural plant that thrives in poor, sandy conditions. The long, strap-like, bluish-green leaves are usually dried and brown at the tip, forming a sharp spine-like point and they are edged with white threads. The reddish-brown flower spikes are often 5-6ft (1.5-1.8m) high and covered with white, bell-shaped blooms. *Y. f.* 'Bright Edge' has a narrow golden margin to the leaf edges, and *Y. f.* 'Variegata' has creamy white ones. Propagate by division, removing and planting rooted suckers in spring.

Zauschneria californica

Californian fuchsia
HEIGHT: 18in (45cm) • Half-hardy
FLOWERING SEASON: Summer/autumn

This clump-forming perennial with a dense, bushy habit, produces bright scarlet, funnel-shaped flowers in clusters at the tips of slender green shoots from late summer onwards. The grey-green leaves are narrow, strap-like and end in a sharp point. The cultivar *Z. c.* ssp. *cana* 'Dublin' has deep, orange-scarlet flowers. Propagation is by division in the spring or semi-ripe cuttings in the summer. Prone to attack by aphids, which cause distorted growth.

More Plants for Dry Sun

There is a wide choice of plants that will thrive in hot dry conditions, particularly those plants which come from the Mediterranean. If you have a sunny aspect and dry beds in your garden the main problem will be moisture loss during the hot summer months. It is a good idea to dig plenty of garden compost and leaf mould into the soil and it is also a help to mulch the bed in summer with wood bark or shavings. Both these measures help the soil to retain moisture and the mulch also suppresses the weeds.

TREES

Carpinus betulus
Juniperus communis
Populus alba

SHRUBS

Abelia × grandiflora
Berberis (in variety)
Buxus sempervirens
Carpentaria californica
Caryopteris × clandonensis
Ceanothus (in variety)
Ceratostigma willmottiana
Cistus × cyprius

Coronilla valentina ssp. *glauca*
Cotoneaster horizontalis
Euonymus fortunei cvs
Fremontodendron 'California Glory'
Hebe pinguifolia 'Pagei'
Hippophae rhamnoides
Indigofera heterantha
Myrtus communis
Olearia × haastii
Philadelphus (in variety)
Phlomis fruticosa
Phygelius capensis (Cape figwort)
Potentilla fruticosa
Rhus typhina
Rosmarinus officinalis
Sambucus (in variety)
Santolina chamaecyparissus
Spirea (in variety)
Symphoricarpus × doorenbosii
Teucrium fruticans

PERENNIALS, GROUND COVER PLANTS & CLIMBERS

Acanthus spinosus
Achillea filipendulina
Anchusa azurea
Artemesia absinthium
Campsis radicans
Carex elata
Catananche centaurea
Centhranthus ruber
Centaurea cyanus (Cornflower)
Clematis tangutica

Crambe cordifolia
Crocosmia 'Lucifer'
Dianthus (in variety)
Eccremocarpus scaber
Euphorbia (in variety)
Geranium (in variety)
Gypsophila (in variety)
Ipomea hederacea
Iris germanica
Kniphofia 'Sunningdale Yellow'
Lamium maculatum
Lonicera japonica 'Halliana'
Lysimachia punctata
Nepeta 'Six Hills Giant'
Nerine (in variety)
Parthenocissus tricuspidata
Phlox paniculata
Phormium tenax
Osteospermum (in variety)
Romneya coulteri
Saponaria ocymoides
Sisyrinchium striatum
Stipa gigantea (Golden Oats)
Thymus herba-barona
Verbascum nigrum
Veronica prostrata
Viola (in variety)
Vitis coignetiae

PLANTS *for* SHADE

Shade-loving plants are essential in most gardens as few are complete-ly without a dark corner or spot under trees. In this selection you can find plants that like damp or dry shade, and also different degrees of shade, from heavy shade to only partial shade.

ABOVE: Alchemilla mollis, *lady's mantle, an invaluable standby for all gardens, was a plant used by Gertrude Jekyll (1843–1932).*

OPPOSITE: *A shady corner is brightened with gold-splashed varieties of holly with the yellow flowers of the perennials like coreopsis and genista (broom) blending in with the yellow rose.*

ABOVE: *A small woodland garden has a handsome* Acer palmatum *var.* dissectum *'Ornatum' as a prominent feature which is underplanted with bluebells.*

RIGHT: Aucuba japonica, *with its yellow-splashed, evergreen leaves, on the right of the picture, will grow even in deep shade, as will the ivies covering the walls and steps. Camellias, on the left, are another plant that grows well in partial shade.*

Very few gardens are completely without shade in some form, but before planting you need to work out whether the shade is dry or damp, since not all plants that do well in damp shade will do well in dry shade and vice versa. Only a tiny number of plants will cope with almost total shade – ivies among them – since all plants require light in some form to create the food they need to survive.

On the whole, shade-loving plants appear rather different from sun-loving ones. They tend to have large foliage – nature's way of ensuring that the maximum amount of chlorophyll is exposed to the light to help photosynthesis (food manufacture) – and with smaller and paler flowers, quite often white. It is possible to create sophisticated and attractive shade gardens using only foliage and white-flowered plants.

This lack of colour was at one time regarded as a disadvantage particularly by the Victorians and Edwardians who preferred the brightest, biggest flowers they could grow in rigidly controlled bedding formations. Gardens that are heavily shaded will not support a bright array of flowering plants – begonias and busy lizzies are among the very few flowering annuals that will survive in shade. They will, however, provide a successful home for many handsome architectural foliage plants and one of the best is *Fatsia japonica* with its big, glossy, evergreen, hand-shaped leaves. Another good performer in quite deep shade is the mottled, green-leaved *Aucuba japonica*. Rhododendrons and azaleas prefer partial shade (but they also like acid soil, so refer to this section as well). Remember that there are many varieties of ivy, with a whole range of different leaf colours and formations

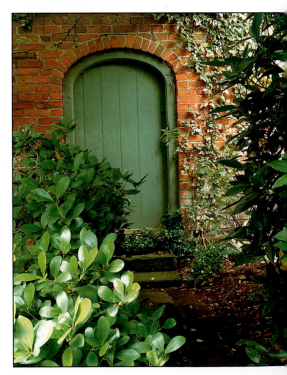

that will grow in even the deepest shade, as will some ferns.

Usually shady areas are to be found under a tree, for example, or beneath a wall. These, because of the canopy of the tree or the shelter of the wall, will also tend to be dry and you must therefore look for plants that like dry shade. Ivies, of course, cope extremely well with dry shade, as do some hostas, foxgloves, hellebores and alchemilla (lady's mantle).

In moist soil in shade you can grow many of the woodland plants, as well as the Welsh poppy (*Meconopsis cambrica*) and some ferns, such as the shuttlecock fern (*Matteuccia struthiopteris*) and the soft shield fern (*Polystichum setiferum*)

Ideally, when creating areas of shade-loving foliage plants, try to contrast the different types, colours and forms of foliage, to

make a green tapestry of leaves. Tall, strappy leaves of sedge can be contrasted with soft feathery fronds of ferns and the big pleated leaves of veratrums, for example. If you have a wide selection of different foliage forms and colours, the garden will acquire just as much interest as a more colourful sunny flower border, and will last throughout the growing season, and into winter if you select a few evergreens as well.

Among good evergreens for the shade garden are the ivies, aucuba and fatsia, mahonia (some of which have the bonus of scented flowers), yew (taxus) and skimmias (again with scented flowers). Skimmias are particularly good for town gardens as they grow slowly.

Many of the plants listed in other sections will flourish in partial shade as well and a comprehensive cross index to the other plants in the book can be found at the end of the chapter.

ABOVE: A shady border, with the front edge in sun, provides a home for ligularias and aucuba, with nasturtiums (tropaeolum) providing front of the border colour. Anthemis tinctoria with its yellow daisy-like heads is on the left.

Aconitum 'Bressingham Spire'

Monkshood/Wolfbane
HEIGHT: 3-5ft (1-1.5m) • Hardy
FLOWERING SEASON: Summer

Known as monkshood or wolfbane, from its hooded flowers, all parts of this plant, from the tuberous roots to the finely divided leaves, are very poisonous. Various aconitum cultivars include: 'Blue Sceptre' and 'Bressingham Spire' which have straight spires about 3ft (1m) tall with deep mauve blue flowers in summer. Needs a moist soil. Cut the flowers down after flowering to encourage flowering stems. Cut down all stems in autumn. Propagate by division in autumn.

Adiantum pedatum

Northern maidenhair fern
HEIGHT: 12in (30cm) • Hardy
FLOWERING SEASON: None

This attractive small fern is native to North America and Japan and is fully hardy in the British Isles, although it dies down soon after the first frosts. The light green fronds with purple stalks arch gracefully from a central rosette. There are several variants: *A. p.* var. *subpumilum*, which is only 5in (12cm) high, is ideal for a rock garden; *A. p.* Asiatic form has copper-coloured fronds in spring, which turn green as they mature. Propagate by sowing the spores in spring, or by dividing the rhizomes in spring. May be attacked by woodlice and root mealy bugs.

Ajuga reptans

Bugle
HEIGHT: 5in (12cm) • Hardy
FLOWERING SEASON: Spring

Known as bugle, this small, vigorous perennial likes shade, although it will grow quite well in sun. It makes good ground cover for damp soil. The dark-leaved cultivars, such as 'Atropurpurea' and 'Braunherz', are among the most attractive. The little spikes of brilliant blue flowers rise above the leaves in spring. It spreads by means of runners. Another cultivar, 'Burgundy Glow', has light blue flowers and cream-edged leaves. Propagate by dividing clumps in winter.

Alchemilla mollis

Lady's mantle
HEIGHT: 18in (45cm) • Hardy
FLOWERING SEASON: Summer

Known as lady's mantle, this perennial has rounded leaves about 5in (13cm) across, with a serrated edge in a downy bluish-green, and it is the foliage which is the plant's chief glory. The lime-green flowers appear in tall sprays in midsummer. It will normally self seed easily, particularly in cracks in paving and grows in all but very boggy soil. A smaller species, *A. alpina*, grows to about 5in (13cm). To propagate, sow seeds under cover in early spring, or divide clumps and replant in autumn and winter.

Begonia rex hybrids

Begonia
HEIGHT: 18-24in (45-60cm) • Tender
FLOWERING SEASON: Insignificant

These evergreen begonias are grown principally for their attractive leaf forms. In general, the leaves are heart-shaped with purple-tinged edges, but different hybrids all have particular characteristics: 'Merry Christmas' has red leaves with an emerald green outer band, while 'Princess of Hanover' has large emerald green leaves with silver and dark red bands. They are ideal for hanging baskets. They require a minimum temperature of 13-15°C (55-59°F), humid conditions, partial shade and moist, slightly acid soil.

Brunnera macrophylla

Siberian bugloss
HEIGHT: 18in (45cm) • Hardy
FLOWERING SEASON: Late spring

The Siberian bugloss bears delicate sprays of small, brilliant, blue flowers, very similar to forget-me-nots, in late spring. These are followed by hairy, heart-shaped, green leaves. The cultivar, *B. m.* 'Hadspen Cream' has green and cream leaves, which tend to colour best in the shady conditions which the plant prefers. Divide the plants in autumn. They are generally trouble-free, but do best in soil that does not dry out in summer. They are fully hardy and make good ground cover plants.

Meconopsis cambrica

Welsh poppy
HEIGHT: 12in (30cm) • Hardy
FLOWERING SEASON: Summer

This perennial, known as the Welsh poppy, produces large, bright, yellow or orange, papery flowers, rather like a large buttercup, all summer long. The plant grows 12–18in (30–45cm) tall and sends up a clump of fresh, green, fern-like foliage surmounted by a number of poppy-like flowers. It flourishes in shady places and needs a light rich soil, preferably neutral to acid, and plenty of water in summer but not very much in winter. It will usually seed itself.

Paeonia lactiflora **hybrids**

Peony
HEIGHT: 2ft (60cm) • Hardy
FLOWERING SEASON: Summer

There are both single and double-flowered forms of this herbaceous perennial and some are scented. Although the double cultivars are more showy, the single cultivars have a particular beauty, especially the pure white cultivars such as *P. l.* 'White Wings' and *P. l.* 'Whitleyi Major'. Grow peonies in a situation sheltered from morning sun, and humus-rich soil. Deadhead after flowering.

Paeonia mlokosewitschii

Peony
HEIGHT: 2ft (60cm) • Hardy
FLOWERING SEASON: Spring

This perennial peony has large, bright, lemon-yellow, single flowers with prominent stamens. The pale green leaves sometimes turn colour in autumn. It also has attractive seedpods. Peonies can be grown in moist, well-drained, well-manured soil in partial shade, ideally sheltered from the morning sun. Plant in early autumn or spring, making sure the crowns are not planted too deep. Prone to some viral disorders and damage from dry soil conditions or root disturbance.

Phyllostachys viridiglaucescens

Bamboo
HEIGHT: 20–25ft (6–8m) • Moderately hardy
FLOWERING SEASON: None

Phyllostachys are useful clump-forming bamboos which come from East Asia and Himalaya. They like moist rich soil which is on the light side and they must have a sheltered position. They flower about once every 30–40 years and after planting the whole plant dies so it is important to save seed when it is available. Propagation is normally by division which should be done in late spring when the new shoots are only an inch or two long. Cut the old shoots right down to the ground in spring.

Polygonatum × hybridum

Solomon's seal
HEIGHT: 4ft (1.2m) • Hardy
FLOWERING SEASON: Summer

Solomon's seal (or David's harp) is a large herbaceous perennial which is tough and very hardy. It will grow almost anywhere in both shade and sun. It makes an attractive arching plant with its thickly ribbed, mid green leaves and tubular white flowers dangling the length of the stems in summer. Give it plenty of leaf-mould, and cut the stems down in autumn. Propagate by division in autumn or spring. Generally disease-free, but sawfly caterpillars may damage leaves.

Schizophragma integrifolium

Hydrangea vine
HEIGHT: 20ft (6m) • Hardy
FLOWERING SEASON: Summer/autumn

This climber will attach itself to a wall or tree trunk using its aerial roots, so it needs no tying in. Closely related to its more vigorous cousin, *S. hydrangeoides*, it has the same large, flat, white florets from summer through to autumn, and bright green leaves with silvery backs. It will grow against a shady wall but does better with some sun. It prefers moist well-drained soil. Propagate by taking short cuttings of the side shoots made with a slight heel of old wood inserted in sandy soil in mid-summer.

Skimmia japonica

Skimmia
HEIGHT: 4ft (1.2m) • Hardy
FLOWERING SEASON: Early summer

This handsome, rounded, bushy shrub is an excellent plant for a small urban garden. It has the bonus not only of neat, glossy evergreen leaves, but of scented, creamy-white flower panicles, followed by bright scarlet berries. It does well in partial shade in good garden soil. The cultivar *S. j.* 'Rubella' with its red rimmed aromatic leaves and red flower buds which open to white flowers in spring is particularly popular. Propagate from semi-ripe cuttings in late summer.

Smilacina racemosa

False spikenard/False Solomon's seal
HEIGHT: 3ft (1m) • Hardy
FLOWERING SEASON: Summer

Known as the false spikenard, or false Solomon's seal, this herbaceous perennial likes lightly shaded woodland and moist, neutral to acid soil. The white scented flowers are carried on the ends of the stems. Cut back the plants in autumn. To propagate, lift the plant in spring and divide the rhizomatous rootstock once the plant has been established for a few years.

Stewartia pseudocamellia

HEIGHT: 16ft (5m) • Hardy
FLOWERING SEASON: Late summer

S. pseudocamellia is a small tree that makes a good subject for planting in part shade in neutral to acid soil. It has single large white cup-shaped flowers in summer and the mid green ovate leaves turn attractive shades of gold and scarlet in autumn, while in winter the peeling bark is a bonus. *S. p.* Koreana Group is similar with flowers that open out flat. *S. sinensis*, has fragrant saucer-shaped flowers. The plant will not flourish against an east wall. Propagate from half-ripe cuttings in late summer.

Symphytum × uplandicum 'Variegatum'

Comfrey
HEIGHT: 10in (25cm) • Hardy
FLOWERING SEASON: Spring

This is a vigorous perennial, which does best in partial shade and fairly moist conditions. They are, perhaps, best suited to a wild garden and generally will self-seed freely. The leaves, which are lance-shaped, are bristly and tough, cream and green splashed, and the flowers are blue or pink. *S. grandiflorum* has small creamy-white flowers and makes good ground cover, *S.* 'Hidcote Blue', is similar with pale blue flowers. Propagate by division in autumn.

Tellima grandiflora

Fringe cup
HEIGHT: 2ft (60cm) • Hardy
FLOWERING SEASON: Early summer

This evergreen perennial is easy to grow and a very good subject for shade. It is a particularly good weed suppressor and makes a good ground cover plant in a shrubbery. The leaves, which form a dense crown close to the ground, are fairly large, maple-like and rough in texture. The tall flower spires carry individually inconspicuous greenish-yellow flowers in early summer. The *Tellima grandiflora* Rubra Group cultivars have bronze purple leaves. Propagate by dividing the plants or by seed.

Thalictrum aquilegiifolium var. album

Meadow rue/Maidenhair fern
HEIGHT: 3-4 ft (1-1.2m) • Hardy
FLOWERING SEASON: Summer

This elegant, clump-forming perennial has particularly attractive foliage, very similar to that of the aquilegia. In summer it carries branching heads of small, white, starry flowers. There is another good white cultivar called 'White Cloud'. *T. aquilegiifolium* has attractive lilac-purple flowers. This plant prefers moist soil, and flourishes in partial shade, although it will also cope with sun. It looks well grown at the edge of woodland. Propagate by division in spring.

Trollius europaeus

Globe flower
HEIGHT: 2ft (60cm) • Hardy
FLOWERING SEASON: Early summer

The globe flower has attractive bright yellow or orange tightly petalled flowers, some 2in (5cm) across. The leaves are deeply divided, lobed and toothed. It does well as a marginal plant for streams or ponds or in any moist soil in sun or partial shade. Good hybrids include the pale yellow *T. × cultorum* 'Canary Bird', or the bright orange *T. × c.* 'Orange Princess'. Cut the flowers back after flowering to produce a second flush of blooms. Divide and replant fibrous roots in autumn.

Veratrum nigrum

Black false hellebore
HEIGHT: 4ft (1.2m) • Hardy
FLOWERING SEASON: Late summer

These big, hardy perennials make handsome spires of deep purple, star-shaped flowers above large, dark green, pleated leaves. They are good imposing plants for the back of a shady border. *V. nigrum* likes moist soil to which peat has been added, and benefits from being cut down in autumn. Propagate by dividing the clumps in autumn or spring. A greenish-white flowered species, *V. album*, makes a similar height and can be treated in the same way.

Viola riviniana **Purpurea Group**

Sweet violet
HEIGHT: 5in (12cm) • Hardy
FLOWERING SEASON: Spring

This small woodland plant formerly known as *V. labradorica purpurea* is ideal for shade. It has attractively coloured purplish-bronze leaves and the typical small, mauve violet flowers in spring. It does well on any light fertile soil which does not dry out. Plant in autumn or spring, and deadhead the flowers as they fade, to encourage a longer flowering season. Can be grown from seed. Pest-free, but prone to a variety of viral disorders.

More Plants for Shade

All gardens have some shade and we have divided the plants that grow best in shade into three groups: plants that will grow in dry shade; plants that will grow in moist shade, of which a number are listed under moisture on page 91; and plants that will grow on a shady wall. These lists are only a selection and there are a number of other plants that are suitable for these problem positions.

PLANTS FOR DRY SHADE

TREES

Acer campestre
  A. platanoides & cvs
Alnus (in variety)
Betula (in variety)
Gleditsia triacanthos
Ilex aquifolium
Robinia pseudoacacia & cvs
Sorbus aucuparia

SHRUBS

Aucuba japonica
Bashania syn. *Arundinaria* (in variety)
Berberis (in variety)
Buxus sempervirens
Cotoneaster horizontalis
Euonymus fortunei cvs

Hippophae rhamnoides
Lonicera pileata
Osmanthus (in variety)
Prunus laurocerasus

PERENNIALS & GROUND COVER PLANTS

Bergenia (in variety)
Iris foetidissima
Lamium maculatum
Pachysandra terminalis
Pulmonaria saccharata

PLANTS FOR MOIST SHADE

TREES

Acers (in variety)
Alnus incana
Betula nigra
  B. pendula
Crateagus (in variety)
Embothrium coccineum
Salix (in variety)
Sorbus aucuparia

SHRUBS

Aucuba japonica
Camellia (in variety)
Clethra arborea
Cornus (in variety)
Desfontainia spinosa
Gaultheria (in variety)
Kalmia latifolia
Leucothoe fontanesiana
Rhododendron (in variety)
Symphoricarpus × doorenbosii

PERENNIALS, GROUND COVER PLANTS & CLIMBERS

Astilbe (in variety)
Begonia rex Hybrids
Campanula lactiflora
Dicentra (in variety)
Dodecatheon pulchellum
Epimedium grandiflorum
Galium odoratum
Houttuynia cordata
Iris pseudacorus
Mentha suavolens
Oxalis acetosella
Polypodium vulgare
Tradescantia (in variety)
Trillium grandiflorum
Tropaeolum speciosum

CLIMBERS & PLANTS FOR SHADY WALLS

Berberidopsis corallina
Clematis (large-flowered varieties)
Cotoneaster horizontalis
Forsythia suspensa
Garrya elliptica
Hydrangea petiolaris
Jasminum nudiflorum (Winter jasmine)
Kerria japonica
Parthenocissus (in variety)
Pyracantha (in variety)
Rosa 'Königin von Dänemark'
  R. 'Madame Legras de Saint German'
  R. 'Maigold'
Schizophragma hydrangeoides

PLANTS
for ACID SOILS

*For gardens, borders and containers with an acid soil, here is a
selection of the many excellent garden plants that prefer this
condition, of which camellias and rhododendrons are perhaps the best
known. Acid soil occurs frequently in areas of high rainfall but can
also be found under conifers where their needles drop.*

ABOVE: Kalmia latifolia, *a magnificent rhododendron-like shrub
which can only be grown successfully in acid soil.*

OPPOSITE: *A mixed heather border. Heathers are ideal for planting in
acid soil and require little upkeep once established.*

ABOVE: *A rich mixture of magnolias and rhododendrons – two of the best candidates for acid soil – makes an enticing late spring display. Some magnolias, however, will grow satisfactorily in alkaline conditions.*

Plants that prefer to grow in an acid soil are often wrongly referred to as ericaceous plants, because many acid-loving plants belong to the family, *Ericaceae*, including heathers (*Erica*), arbutus, kalmia, pieris and, of course, rhododendrons. It is worth remembering that many other attractive plants such as camellia, eucryphia, hamamelis and some magnolias are also acid-loving but are not of the family *Ericaceae*. The correct term for plants which prefer acid soil is calcifuges.

Some excellent garden plants grow only in acid soil, so if your garden has this condition, you can look forward to growing some real treasures. Acid-loving plants are often associated with the tendency to be spring flowering as are camellias and hamamelis, but many of these plants, for example fothergilla and stewartia, are renowned for their autumn foliage colour, and if you can grow a range of heathers it is possible to have plants in flower practically all year round.

You can check on the pH of your soil to determine its acidity by using a home soil testing kit. It is a matter of a few minutes to discover whether or not your soil is suitable. As a rough guide, if your soil measures more than 6.5 on the pH scale it is unsuitable for growing acid-lovers. Of course, even if this is the case, you can always grow the plants you want in containers where you have complete control over the growing medium.

In nature, the most acid soils are usually found on heather moorland, or in coniferous forests. Remember, soil type is not always directly linked to soil pH. Acid soils can be free-draining and sandy, or heavy and sticky, or even organic with a high peat content. Clay soils may be acid or alkaline, depending on their make-up. Peat-based soils are almost always acid. Some soils, even if originally alkaline, can gradually become more acid as a result of the lime being washed out of the upper layers, close to the soil surface. This is due to the fact that rainwater is slightly acidic, and the lime in the soil dissolves and is washed (leached) down through the soil. Soils in high rainfall areas are more likely to be acid than alkaline and many of the gardens famous for their rhododendrons are found in these areas.

Plants which grow naturally in acid soils, marked pH in the text, will usually struggle when grown in anything else. This is because of the different availability of plant nutrients at lower pH levels as plants vary in their ability to absorb these nutrients. Most acid-loving plants are unable to take up enough iron from the soil if the pH is too high. Initially, this shows as a yellowing (chlorosis) between the leaf veins, and in many cases is followed by the death of the plant unless additional iron is supplied.

LEFT: *Heathers are ideal subjects for acid soils, and when mixed together in a large bed, provide a wonderful tapestry of colour and shape. The best impact is gained when, as here, several different cultivars are combined in one area of the garden.*

Abies koreana

Korean fir
HEIGHT: 10ft (3m) • Hardy
FLOWERING SEASON: None

Commonly known as the Korean fir, this conifer is a small, slow-growing tree, with a broad-based, conical shape, the base of the tree being as wide as its overall height. Each leaf or 'needle' is an attractive dark green above with a silvery white underside. It produces striking, violet-purple cones 2-3in (5-7.5cm) long, even on young plants. Propagation is by seed, sown into pots and placed outdoors in late winter. Prone to attack by the adelgid, which distorts young growths.

Acer rubrum

Red maple
HEIGHT: 50ft (15m) • Hardy
FLOWERING SEASON: Spring

The red maple forms a large round-headed deciduous tree with dark green leaves which turn bright red in the autumn. There are tiny red flowers which appear on the branches in the spring but these are insignificant. Like all maples the best autumn colour is found when the tree is grown on acid soil but it is easy to cultivate and flourishes in any ordinary well-tilled soil.

Andromeda polifolia 'Compacta'

HEIGHT: 6-9in (15-23cm) • Hardy • pH
FLOWERING SEASON: Late summer/early autumn

This charming dwarf evergreen shrub has slender stems covered in narrow, bluish-green leaves each with a white underside. The soft pink flowers are produced in clusters on the tips of the shoots. It belongs to the heather family and grows wild in peat bogs in northern Europe. It does not flourish when there is lime in the soil. Propagate by semi-ripe cuttings taken in late summer. The plant may suffer from vine weevil grubs, which eat the roots and cause wilting and collapse if they attack in large numbers.

Arbutus × andrachnoides

HEIGHT: 50ft (15m) • Hardy
FLOWERING SEASON: Late autumn/early spring

A hybrid between *A. andrachos* and *A. unedo*, the Killarney strawberry tree, this attractive, slow-growing, broad-leafed evergreen forms an open spreading tree with striking orange-red bark which peels and flakes from the trunk and older branches to reveal the new bark beneath. The white, urn-shaped flowers, produced in large upright spikes in late autumn/early spring appear as the orange-red fruits of the previous year ripen. In a severe winter some of the leaves and shoots may be damaged. Propagation is by semi-ripe cuttings taken in late summer.

Arctostaphylos uva-ursi

Bearberry
HEIGHT: 4in (10cm) • Hardy • pH
FLOWERING SEASON: Summer

This is a low evergreen shrub with a spreading habit and small, oval, bright green leaves, that is ideal as a ground-cover plant. The small heather-like flowers are white flushed pink, followed by a display of small scarlet berries in autumn and winter. It likes acid soil and shelter from cold winds. A particularly interesting form is *A. u.* 'Point Reyes', which has pale pink flowers against a backdrop of grey-green leaves. Propagation is by semi-ripe cuttings with a heel taken in late summer and inserted into a cold frame.

Aristolochia durior

Birthwort/Dutchman's pipe
HEIGHT: 27ft (9m) • Not fully hardy
FLOWERING SEASON: Summer

A vigorous climber, its unusual tubular flowers are yellowish-green with a brownish-purple interior, they are 1.5-2in (3-5cm) long with the bottom half bent upwards to resemble a smoker's pipe, hence the common name Dutchman's pipe. The large, dull green leaves are heart-shaped and up to 12in (30cm) in length, borne on thin, woody twining stems. It provides a good wall covering when given support. Propagation is by softwood tip cuttings taken in July. Thin shoots in early spring.

Fothergilla major

HEIGHT: 6ft (1.8m) • Hardy • pH
FLOWERING SEASON: Spring

This is a slow-growing shrub with a thin straggly appearance. The broadly oval leaves are a glossy dark-green on the upper surface, with a bluish-white bloom beneath. In the autumn they turn yellow and vivid orange-red before the winter frosts. The flowers, which are very fragrant and look like small, white bottle-brushes, appear before the leaves. They prefer sandy, lime-free soil and a sheltered position. Propagation is by layering young shoots in autumn. Prone to damage and branch death by the coral spot fungus.

Gaultheria mucronata

HEIGHT: 3ft (1m) • Hardy • pH
FLOWERING SEASON: Late spring/early summer

Formerly known as pernettyas, gaultherias are a genus of evergreen shrubs. *G. mucronata* has small, glossy, dark green leaves which are oval and end in a sharp point. The flowers are generally white, followed by clusters of small round fruit, which vary from white and pink to purple and red. Cultivars include: *G. m.* 'Bell's Seedling' which has cherry-red fruits and *G. m.* 'Lilacina', with pale lilac fruit. Male and female plants are needed for berries. Propagation is by semi-ripe cuttings taken in early autumn.

Gaultheria shallon

Shallon
HEIGHT: 4ft (1.2m) • Hardy • pH
FLOWERING SEASON: Late spring/early summer

This vigorous evergreen plant produces broad, oval leaves which are thick, leathery and borne on slender, upright, reddish-green stems. The small, pinkish-white flowers which are produced at the base of the leaves and form large drooping clusters, are followed by dark purple fruits in the autumn. This plant is very invasive and requires plenty of room, but it is ideal for growing in shade, and makes excellent ground cover. Propagate by dividing established plants in winter.

Gentiana sino-ornata

Gentian
HEIGHT: 6in (15cm) • Hardy • pH ·
FLOWERING SEASON: Autumn

This evergreen perennial is possibly the best autumn-flowering gentian. In the spring a number of thin green trailing stems appear which sprawl across the ground, each of which, lengthening during the summer, produces in the autumn a brilliant blue flower, handsomely striped on the outside. *G. sino-ornata* needs moist, acid soil. Propagation is by 'thongs', where the roots, complete with a small segment of stem, are pulled from the parent plant and potted on or replanted in early spring.

Halesia monticola

Snowdrop tree/Silver bell tree
HEIGHT: 25ft (8m) • Hardy
FLOWERING SEASON: Spring

A hardy, deciduous tree which has a spreading habit, this attractive plant is grown primarily for its distinctive clusters of white, bell-shaped flowers, which appear in spring before the leaves. The flowers are usually followed by small, green, winged and roughly pear-shaped fruit in the autumn. The broadly oval leaves are a light to mid green. The tree prefers moist acid to neutral soil and propagation is by softwood cuttings taken in summer or by seed sown in a cold frame in autumn.

Hamamelis × intermedia

Witch hazel
HEIGHT: 10ft (3m) • Hardy
FLOWERING SEASON: Winter/spring

This very distinctive and beautiful deciduous shrub produces its fragrant flowers in winter. They have small strap-like petals chiefly in shades of yellow, although some cultivars have darker flowers: *H. × intermedia* 'Ruby Glow' has copper-red flowers and *H. × i.* 'Diane' deep red ones. They prefer sun or semi-shade and well-drained acid to neutral soil. The large, mid green leaves are broadly oval and give a magnificent autumn display. Propagation is by softwood cuttings in late summer or grafting in midwinter.

Holboellia coriacea

HEIGHT: 18ft (6m) • Moderately hardy
FLOWERING SEASON: Late spring

An evergreen climber that supports itself by means of twining woody stems carrying glossy green leaves composed of three subdivided stalked leaflets. The flowers of both sexes are borne on the same plant; the male flowers are purple and the female ones are greenish-white with purple tints. As a result, in the autumn, blackish-purple, sausage-shaped fruits containing black seeds usually develop. It grows in any well-drained soil in sun or semi-shade. Propagate by semi-ripe stem cuttings taken in late summer.

Hydrangea macrophylla 'Générale Vicomtesse de Vibray'

HEIGHT: 5ft (1.5m) • Moderately hardy
FLOWERING SEASON: Summer/autumn

Mop-head (hortensias) and lace-cap hydrangeas have broad, flat blooms, which in lace-caps are surrounded by one or more rows of pink, white or blue sepals. They grow in most soils but the colour varies from pink to blue according to the amount of acid in the soil. As their name implies they like moisture. Remove the dead flower heads in spring after the frosts and cut up one third of the shoots on mature plants to ground level. Take stem cuttings in late summer.

Indigofera heterantha

Indigo
HEIGHT: 5ft (1.5m) • Moderately hardy
FLOWERING SEASON: Early summer/autumn

A charming member of the pea family, this plant produces spikes of purplish-pink flowers on arching branches throughout the summer. It prefers well-drained loamy soil and a sunny position. The plant can be grown against a wall as a climber or in open ground where it should be cut back in the spring. If cut down by frosts it will regenerate. Propagate by cuttings of young shoots taken in mid-summer and inserted in a cold frame or by seed in late spring.

Kalmia latifolia

Calico bush
HEIGHT: 10ft (3m) • Hardy • pH
FLOWERING SEASON: Summer

A magnificent rhododendron-like evergreen shrub with a dense bushy habit, the alternate leaves, which are a glossy dark green and have a tough leathery appearance, are borne on thin, whippy, green stems. The unusual crimped buds open to produce large clusters of bright pink, cup-shaped flowers in summer. The cultivars *K. l.* var. *alba* and *K. l.* 'Silver Dollar' have white flowers flushed pink. It prefers full sun and moist acid soil. Propagation is by semi-ripe stem cuttings taken in late summer.

Kirengeshoma palmata

HEIGHT: 3ft (1m) • Hardy • pH
FLOWERING SEASON: Late summer/autumn

An upright hardy herbaceous perennial which has lush, bright green, maple-like leaves. The creamy-yellow, shuttlecock-shaped flowers are produced in clusters above the large, roundish leaves on tall, erect purplish-maroon stems and appear in late summer. This plant does best in conditions where there is some light shade with protection from the wind, while a damp but well-drained, preferably lime-free, soil is essential. It should be planted in the spring and propagation is by division of the rootstock in early spring.

Koelreuteria paniculata

Golden-rain tree/Pride of India
HEIGHT: 30ft (9m) • Moderately hardy
FLOWERING SEASON: Late summer

A handsome deciduous tree with large mid green leaves divided into numerous leaflets which turn yellow in autumn. It has large terminal clusters of yellow flowers in late summer followed by inflated triangular pinkish-brown seed pods and requires a position in full sun and well-drained, fertile soil. It is best propagated by seeds sown when ripe in the autumn in sandy soil in a cold frame. The tree is named after Joseph G Koelreuter, a professor of natural history at Karlsruhe in the eighteenth century.

Leucothoe fontanesiana

HEIGHT: 5ft (1.5m) • Hardy • pH
FLOWERING SEASON: Spring

An elegant evergreen shrub which is ideal as
ground cover. The graceful, arching shoots
carry leathery, strap-like leaves, which are a
glossy dark green in the spring and summer,
becoming tinted a beetroot-red or bronze in
autumn and winter. The small white flowers
are urn-shaped and hang in small clusters
along the entire length of the stem.
L. f. 'Rainbow' has leaves splashed with
cream, yellow and pink. Likes moist acid soil
and shade or partial shade. Propagation is by
semi-ripe cuttings taken in late summer.

Liquidambar styraciflua 'Worplesdon'

Sweet gum
HEIGHT: 25ft (8m) • Hardy
FLOWERING SEASON: Spring

A large tree with maple-like, glossy, dark
green leaves which turn orange and yellow
in autumn. Initially forming a slender
pyramid with the lower branches having
upturned ends, it develops a broadly conical
shape with age. The trunk becomes deeply
grooved and fissured, changing from dark
brown to dark grey. Small green flowers
may be produced in spring. Propagation is
by grafting under protection in spring.

Lupinus luteus

Yellow lupin
HEIGHT: 2½ft (75cm) • Hardy
FLOWERING SEASON: Summer

This striking annual has mid green stems
thickly covered with soft hairs, the pale to
mid green oval leaves are narrower towards
the base and sparsely covered in a coating
of fine soft hair. The bright yellow flowers,
which are arranged in a circle or whorl at the
end of the stem, are followed by small, black,
hairy pods, each containing about five slightly flattened black seeds. Propagation is by
seed sown in situ in the spring; pre-soak the
seed in water for about twenty-four hours.

Magnolia × soulangeana 'Lennei'

Magnolia/Lily tree
HEIGHT: 20ft (6m) • Hardy
FLOWERING SEASON: Early spring

Contrary to opinion there are a number of
magnolias which will tolerate chalky
(alkaline) soil, *M. delavayi, M. kobus* and
M. wilsonii are three of them. That said the
majority thrive best in neutral to acid soil
and like to be sheltered from cold winds
which may otherwise damage the flowers
when they emerge in the spring. The
× *soulangeana* hybrids like 'Lennei' are among
the hardiest and have a colour range of pink
through rose-purple to white.

Magnolia stellata

Star magnolia
HEIGHT: 10ft (3m) • Hardy
FLOWERING SEASON: Spring

The star magnolia is a shapely bush which
carries many fragrant, star-like, white flowers
in great profusion in spring before coming
into leaf. The leaves are narrow and deep
green. Magnolias come from North
America, the Himalayas and Japan and are
named after Pierre Magnol. Among the
finest are *M. campbellii, M. acuminata* (the
cucumber tree), *M denudata* (the lily tree)
and *M. grandiflora* (page 148). They can be
propagated by semi-ripe cuttings taken in
summer or by seed sown in autumn.

Meconopsis betonicifolia

Blue poppy
HEIGHT: 4ft (1.2m) • Hardy
FLOWERING SEASON: Summer

The mid green leaves are oblong in shape
and covered with soft bristles. The vivid,
sky-blue flowers, with their central core of
golden-yellow stamens, are carried on tall,
slender stems, in hairy, pod-like buds. This
plant requires a deep, rich, preferably acid
compost and a cool, sheltered, shady site.
Propagate this perennial from seed, sown
into a cold frame in the autumn, and kept
sheltered over winter. Do not allow these
plants to flower in the first year after germi-
nation and divide them every four years.

Menziesia ciliicalyx 'Spring Morning'

HEIGHT: 3-5ft (1-1.5m) • Hardy • pH
FLOWERING SEASON: Early summer

This very attractive flowering shrub is a native of Japan and is a real treasure when grown in association with rhododendrons. The leaves are pale to mid green in colour and have a bristled margin. *M. c.* 'Spring Morning' has pale creamy urn-shaped flowers while *M. 'c.* var. *purpurea* has purple ones. They appear during late spring and early summer. It likes semi-shade and moist acid soil. Take semi-ripe cuttings with a heel during mid to late summer.

Ourisia macrophylla

HEIGHT: 10in (25cm) • Hardy
FLOWERING SEASON: Midsummer

A low-growing plant with creeping rhizomatous rootstocks below ground, and mid green rounded leaves with a notched margin that form dense mats. This plant produces erect, slender stems, which carry white (sometimes streaked with pink) tubular flowers up to 1in (2.5cm) long, very like those of a miniature penstemon, on a spike above the leaves. This plant must have partial shade and a well-drained soil. Propagation is by division in spring or by seed sown in late spring.

Oxydendrum arboreum

Sorrel tree
HEIGHT: 27ft (9m) • Hardy • pH
FLOWERING SEASON: Summer

This deciduous spreading tree is grown mainly for its spectacular yellow and crimson autumn leaf colours. In spring and summer they are elliptical in shape and a glossy dark green. The white flowers are produced in long, dangling clusters on the tips of the shoots in summer. In winter the bark is an attractive rusty-red, which turns to grey as it ages. It likes sun and moist acid soil. Propagation is by softwood cuttings taken in summer or by fresh seed sown in autumn.

Picea pungens 'Koster'

Colorado spruce
HEIGHT: 50ft (15m) • Hardy
FLOWERING SEASON: Spring

The type forms a medium-sized tree with a conical profile. New growth is orange-brown, while the sharply pointed mature 'needles' are greyish-green. The dangling light-brown cones are bluish-green when young. The most popular cultivar, *P. p.* 'Koster', forms a small tree with silvery-blue leaves. Most species can be propagated by seed sown outdoors in the spring, the named selections are grafted under cover in early spring. Prone to attack by the adelgid, which sucks sap and distorts young growths.

Pieris japonica 'Firecrest'

HEIGHT: 10ft (3m) • Hardy • pH
FLOWERING SEASON: Spring

These compact evergreen shrubs have narrow leaves and white or pink bell-shaped flowers that look much like lily-of-the-valley. Most are grown for their spring display of bright foliage, ranging from lime-green to crimson or bronze. They like a shady site and moist acid soil. The cultivar *Pieris* 'Forest Flame' has young leaves which start red, change through pink and cream before turning green. *P. j.* 'Variegata' is a slow-growing cultivar with white and green variegated leaves, flushed pink when young. Propagation is by semi-ripe cuttings in late summer.

Pseudolarix amabilis

Golden larch
HEIGHT: 45ft (15m) • Hardy • pH
FLOWERING SEASON: Insignificant

This is a beautiful, deciduous and open-crowned tree that is very slow-growing, partly because the growing tips of young trees are often killed by late spring frosts, yet will eventually make a good height. The long, larch-like leaves are light green and turn a clear golden-yellow, orange and then reddish-brown in autumn. It bears erect cones with spreading scales which carry the seeds. This plant is particularly sensitive to lime in the soil. Propagation is by seed sown under protection in spring.

Pseudotsuga menziesii

Douglas fir
HEIGHT: 75ft (25m) • Hardy
FLOWERING SEASON: Insignificant

This large vigorous tree develops a deeply grooved, corky bark as it ages, and a flat, broadly spreading crown also develops as the tree reaches maturity. The broad 'needle' leaves are aromatic and arranged in two horizontal lines along the branchlets, they are a rich dark green above with two silvery lines on the underside. The blue-leaved variety, *P. m.* var. *glauca,* will tolerate drier soils. Propagate by seed sown under protection in spring.

Rhododendron 'Kirin'

Azalea
HEIGHT: 5ft (1.5m) • Hardy • pH
FLOWERING SEASON: Spring

Botanically speaking all azaleas are classified as rhododendrons but most gardeners commonly reserve the name of azalea for those species which lose their leaves in winter. Just to complicate things a number of azaleas are evergreen and 'Kirin' is one of those. All rhododendrons and azaleas prefer moist, neutral to acid soil, with some dappled shade. Propagate by half-ripe cuttings taken with a thin heel from the current year's growth in mid-summer or by layering.

Rhododendron davidsonianum

Rhododendron
HEIGHT: 5-10ft (1.5-3m) • Hardy • pH
FLOWERING SEASON: Late spring

Rhododendrons in full bloom are one of the most glorious sights of spring and the best known gardens, Kew, the Savill Garden, Exbury and Bodnant in England are well worth visiting to appreciate the massed blooms. *R. davidsonianum* is a relatively slow growing species with clusters of pale pink to pale mauve funnel-shaped flowers. As all rhododendrons are shallow rooting it is a good idea to mulch with half-decayed leaves in late spring to keep the soil moist in summer.

Rhodohypoxis baurii

HEIGHT: 4in (10cm) • Not fully hardy
FLOWERING SEASON: Spring/summer

This low-growing herbaceous perennial has a tufty habit and a crown of erect, spear-shaped hairy leaves. The small, flattish, six-petalled flowers, which vary from white to pale pink or red, are carried on slender, erect stems, each flower has six petals which meet at the centre so the flower has no eye. The ideal conditions for this plant are full sun and a moist, sandy, peaty soil. Propagation can be achieved by seed sown in spring for the species, but named cultivars, such as *R. b.* 'Douglas', must be propagated by division in early spring.

Staphylea colchica

Bladder nut
HEIGHT: 11ft (3.5m) • Hardy
FLOWERING SEASON: Late spring

A large deciduous shrub which comes from the Causasus which bears clusters of white flowers in late spring. These are followed by inflated seed pods up to 2in (5cm) long. It has bright green leaves each having three to five oval leaflets, and requires sun or semi-shade and moist fertile soil. *S. holocarpa* 'Rosea' has pink flowers. The species can be propagated by seed sown in autumn and selected forms by softwood cuttings taken with a slight heel of old wood in mid-summer. Trim young plants to encourage a bushy habit.

Stewartia sinensis

HEIGHT: 20ft (6m) • Hardy
FLOWERING SEASON: Summer

This small deciduous tree has attractive brown stems and unusually peeling ornamental bark; it belongs to the camellia family. The broad, spear-shaped, mid green leaves have a leathery texture and provide a vivid display of red and yellow in the autumn. The pure white, cup-shaped flowers have prominent yellow anthers in the centre. These plants grow best in a sunny spot with their roots shaded, and are very intolerant of root disturbance. Propagation is by softwood cuttings taken in the summer, or by seed sown in a cold frame in autumn.

Styrax officinalis

Storax
HEIGHT: 12ft (4m) • Hardy • pH
FLOWERING SEASON: Early summer

This attractive deciduous shrub has a loose, open habit and spear-shaped leaves that are dark green on the upper surface and silver-white beneath. The short drooping clusters of large, white, fragrant, bell-shaped flowers are carried on the tips of the shoots in early summer. This plant prefers a sheltered position in full sun or partial shade, and a moist well-drained soil. Propagation is by softwood cuttings taken in summer, or by seed sown in a cold frame in autumn.

Taxodium distichum

Bald cypress/Swamp cypress
HEIGHT: 75ft (25m) • Hardy
FLOWERING SEASON: Winter

A strikingly beautiful, slow-growing deciduous tree which has fibrous, reddish-brown, peeling bark. The branches are a bright orange-brown with grey-green young shoots. The bright yellow-green leaves are small and narrow, turning a russet brown in autumn. This tree is ideal for growing close to water, so that the beautiful autumn colours are reflected on the surface. Propagation is by seed sown in spring or by hardwood cuttings taken in autumn.

Trillium grandiflorum

Trinity flower/Wood lily/Wake robin
HEIGHT: 18in (45cm) • Hardy
FLOWERING SEASON: Spring/summer

This clump-forming perennial develops into a dome-shaped plant with large, oval, deeply veined, dark green leaves. The pure white, funnel-shaped flowers, which gradually become flushed pink as the flower ages, are produced singly on short arching stems from spring until summer. There are also species with pink flowers and double white flowers. It likes shade and moist soil. Propagation is by division of the rhizomes after the leaves have died down.

Tropaeolum speciosum

Flame creeper
HEIGHT: 15ft (4.5m) • Hardy
FLOWERING SEASON: Summer/autumn

This deciduous herbaceous perennial climber has long-stalked, brilliant scarlet, trumpet-shaped flowers which are made up of five rounded wavy petals opening out flat, produced singly on curling stems. The stems, with their notched and circular mid green leaves, form an attractive plant even before the flowers start to appear. These plants are slow to establish but are worth the wait and like to have their roots in the shade. Prune in spring by cutting out the dead stems. Propagate by division in early spring.

Tsuga heterophylla

Western hemlock
HEIGHT: 70-100ft (20-30m) • Hardy
FLOWERING SEASON: None

A large, fast-growing tree with drooping branches and shoot tips. The young shoots are white and hairy bearing leaves which are dark green above and silver on the underside. The dark brown bark is scaly and deeply grooved. These trees perform best in sheltered areas with a heavy rainfall and in a partially shaded position. Propagation is by seed sown under protection in the spring, or for named cultivars, by semi-ripe cuttings taken in autumn. Other species are smaller. They dislike urban pollution.

Uvularia grandiflora

Bellwort/Merry-bells
HEIGHT: 18in (45cm) • Hardy • pH
FLOWERING SEASON: Spring

This clump-forming herbaceous perennial has narrow, pointed leaves which appear in the spring and only partially unfold to reveal clusters of graceful, bell-shaped, yellow flowers. These are carried on olive-green, succulent-looking stems, and after flowering the leaves unroll completely. A slower-growing species, *U. perfoliata*, has yellow flowers with twisted petals. Semi-shade is essential for this plant and it prefers moist peaty soil. Propagation is by division in early spring before flowering.

Vaccinium corymbosum

Blueberry/Whortleberry/Cowberry/Bilberry
HEIGHT: 5ft (1.5m) • Hardy • pH
FLOWERING SEASON: Spring

This small deciduous shrub forms a dense suckering thicket of upright multi-branched shoots, covered in bright green, spear-shaped leaves, which turn to bronze and scarlet in the autumn. The flowers are urn-shaped and vary in colour from white to white-blushed-pink. They are followed in the autumn by sweet, edible, black berries which are covered by blue bloom. *V. c.* 'Pioneer' is grown for its vivid red autumn foliage. Propagation is by semi-ripe cuttings taken in late summer.

Viburnum plicatum 'Mariesii'

HEIGHT: 6ft (1.8m) • Hardy
FLOWERING SEASON: Spring/summer

This is a spectacular, large, wide-spreading shrub with a tendency to produce its branches in stacked layers, which gives a tiered effect. The oval leaves, which are deeply crinkled and a bright green through the summer, change to yellow and reddish-purple in autumn. The white flowers are carried in large flat heads, making the shrub look as if a layer of snow has just fallen on it. Propagation is by semi-ripe cuttings taken in late summer or by layering young shoots in early autumn.

Zenobia pulverulenta

Zenobia
HEIGHT: 6ft (1.8m) • Hardy • pH
FLOWERING SEASON: Summer

This is a beautiful small deciduous or semi-evergreen shrub with an open habit and thin, twiggy stems that are covered in a bluish-white bloom. The strap-like leaves are a glossy blue-green with a bluish-white underside when young. Large white flowers, very similar to those of the lily-of-the-valley, that hang in clusters from the leaf joints are produced in summer. The blooms give off a faint scent of aniseed. Propagation is by semi-ripe cuttings taken in late summer.

More Plants for Acid Soils

It is important to distinguish between those plants which are lime-haters and have to have acid soil to thrive and other plants which are quite tolerant of some acidity in the soil. The lime-haters are marked pH in the plant details and if you garden on clay or chalk (limestone) it really is a waste of time trying to grow them.

Otherwise if your soil is not too acid and your climate isn't too wet then there is very little restriction on what you can grow. Your roses may not be quite as bountiful, and your stone fruit may not yield quite as much as someone who lives a hundred miles away and is lucky enough to garden on the best loam but they will be fine for the average gardener. You may be best to avoid the Mediterranean plants like cistus and lavender. Acid soil can always be sweetened by adding lime and the productivity improved by digging in compost or manure.

The following plants included in other chapters in this book are just some of those that can also be grown in acid soils. Space prevents the inclusion of roses and bulbs which are also perfectly viable.

TREES

Acers (in variety)
Alnus incana
Amelanchier canadensis
Carpinus betulus
Chamaecyparis lawsoniana (and most conifers)
Crataegus (in variety)
Fagus (in variety)
Hamamelis mollis
Larix decidua
Liriodendron tulipifera
Magnolia grandiflora
Sorbus (in variety)

SHRUBS

Aucuba japonica
Berberis (in variety)
Ceanothus (in variety)
Choisya ternata
Cornus (in variety)
Cotinus coggygria
Euonymus fortunei cvs
Forsythia suspensa
Lavatera 'Barnsley'
Ligustrum ovalifolium
Mahonia (in variety)
Osmanthus (in variety)
Rhododendron – including *azaleas* (in variety)
Sambucus (in variety)
Sarcococca (in variety)
Syringa (in variety)
Vaccinium glaucoalbum
Viburnum (in variety)

PERENNIALS, GROUND COVER PLANTS & CLIMBERS

Aconitum 'Bressingham Spire'
Alchemilla mollis
Aquilegia alpina
Aronia arbutifolia
Artemesia absinthium
Aruncus dioicus
Astrantia major
Bergenia cordifolia
Buddleja (in variety)
Campanula (in variety)
Centhranthus ruber
Ceratostigma willmottianum
Echinops bannaticus
Filipendula palmata
Galium odoratum
Geranium (in variety)
Gunnera manicata
Iris germanica
Jasminum officinale
Lamium maculatum
Lapageria rosea
Ligularia (in variety)
Myosotis sylvestris
Phlomis fruticosa
Polygonatum × *hybridum*
Primula (in variety)
Santolina chamaecyparissus
Tradescantia (in variety)
Veronica prostrata
Vinca minor 'Argenteovariegata'
Viola (in variety)

PLANTS *for* ALKALINE SOILS

Chalky (alkaline) soil occurs in limestone areas, but is also created by the inclusion of builder's rubble in the soil, often around the bases of walls, where clematis thrives. Although gardeners with this soil are fortunate in that lime-loving plants are more numerous than acid-loving plants, chalky (alkaline) dry soil does need added leaf mould and compost to increase the nutrient content and water-retaining capacity.

ABOVE: Saponaria ocymoides, *with the charming common name of 'Tumbling Ted', is an ideal mat-forming perennial for a dry bank.*

OPPOSITE: *An informal border of yarrow, violas, geraniums and iris makes an attractive display. Most of the summer-flowering perennials do well on chalky (alkaline) soil, giving a wide range to choose from.*

ABOVE: Linum narbonense *is a charming, small, clump-forming perennial with flowers ranging from light to deep blue in summer. It likes light soil.*

It is understandable that those gardeners who can grow rhododendrons, and the many other lovely plants needing similar soil, think they are so lucky, but if you look at the vast range of lime-loving plants available, you will soon realize that as a group they can provide interest and beauty at least on a par with the acid-loving plants.

Plants that prefer to grow in an alkaline soil, that is, with a pH of 7.0 or higher, are called calcicole plants. Use a soil-testing kit to check your soil's pH. If you look at the number of plants which grow well on alkaline soils, you will see that there is a wide range of attractive trees and shrubs, including clematis, lonicera (honeysuckle), sorbus and viburnums, that like these conditions. The list of plants also includes many herbaceous perennials, and many members of the pea family often excel on these soils, including cytisus and genista (broom), gleditsia, lathyrus (the sweet pea), and robinia.

In some areas, gardens made up of a shallow layer of soil over solid chalk or limestone have several characteristic features which make them difficult to garden. The presence of the base rock so near the surface of the soil makes it difficult to position plants at any depth without resorting to the use of a pickaxe or other heavy-duty implement. Even this does not alter the fact that you are planting into rock and not soil, so that plant roots will have great difficulty penetrating it. This can lead to poor anchorage, particularly of trees, although some trees like beech (*Fagus sylvatica*), which does grow on shallow, chalky (alkaline) soil, have developed a naturally broad, shallow root system in order to cope with the lack of soil.

During dry periods, these thin layers of soil can hold only limited reserves of water, and the upper levels of the rock become extremely dry. However, once established, many plants will produce an extensive root system which penetrates the soft rock, so that when rain does fall, they can absorb the maximum amount before it drains through the soil. Adding bulky organic matter to improve the soil is usually best done soon after a period of rain.

Many gardens have certain areas with more chalky (alkaline) soil than other parts, in particular where builder's rubble has accumulated, often near house walls or patios. This is particularly true of many town gardens in areas around garden walls where old lime mortar may turn the soil from acid to alkaline. In a case like this, move plants if they do not do well in the position chosen for them originally. These are ideal situations for chalk- (limestone-) loving plants, especially clematis, but it is essential when growing clematis that you shelter their roots from hot sun. Many gardeners are frightened of moving plants, particularly in summer. Even if it is not recommended, if you take plenty of soil with the plant, dig a deep hole, and puddle the plant in thoroughly, it is usually perfectly satisfactory.

ABOVE: *An informal woodland walk in spring in a garden with chalky (alkaline) soil. Hellebores seen on the left do best in partial shade.*

LEFT: *The glorious rugosa rose, R. 'Roseraie de L'Haÿ' will flourish in chalky (alkaline) soil. It is sometimes grown successfully as a low hedge.*

Acanthus spinosus

Bear's breeches
HEIGHT: 3ft (1m) • Hardy
FLOWERING SEASON: Summer

This herbaceous perennial is often described as an 'architectural' plant. It has large arching leaves, which are a glossy dark-green and strap-like, with sharp spines on the points of the toothed margins. The tall spikes of white and purple tubular flowers, which alternate between layers of green spiny bracts, are borne throughout summer. The dead flowerheads look attractive during winter when frost-covered. Propagate by root cuttings in early spring, or division in winter.

Acer negundo 'Flamingo'

Ash-leaved maple/Box elder
HEIGHT: 50ft (15m) • Hardy
FLOWERING SEASON: Spring

A vigorous tree with ash-like leaves that are bright green in summer, turning to golden-yellow in autumn. In the spring, bright greenish-yellow flowers are produced in flat clusters on the branches before the leaves. *A. n.* var. *violaceum* has purple leaves and shoots, and the cultivar *A. n.* 'Variegatum' has mid green leaves marbled with creamy-white flecks and pink shoot tips in the spring. Propagation is by seed sown in the spring or budding in the summer (for cultivars).

Achillea filipendulina 'Gold Plate'

Yarrow
HEIGHT: 3ft (1m) • Hardy
FLOWERING SEASON: Late summer/early autumn

This herbaceous perennial has a compact upright habit, with broad, finely divided, slightly hairy, dull green leaves. The lemon-yellow flowers are held erect above the foliage in bold flat clusters 5-6in (12-15cm) across. The cultivar *A. f.* 'Gold Plate' has deep golden-yellow flowers. Propagate by lifting the clumps in early spring, dividing them into smaller portions of 4-5 shoots and replanting them in the growing site.

Actinidia kolomikta

HEIGHT: 12ft (4m) • Hardy
FLOWERING SEASON: Late summer

This deciduous climbing shrub with twining stems has heart-shaped, dark green leaves marked with pink and white at the tip. Actinidias generally prefer shade but *A. kolomikta* will grow well on a sheltered fence or wall in full sun and preferably a neutral, well-drained soil. It has small white, slightly fragrant flowers in June. The young leaves are prone to damage by late spring frosts. Propagation is by semi-ripe cuttings in mid- and late summer. In late winter prune by thinning out overcrowded growths, and shorten excessively vigorous shoots.

Aesculus pavia

Red buckeye/Horse chestnut
HEIGHT: 10ft (3m) • Hardy
FLOWERING SEASON: Early summer

This is a round-headed shrub, with large, mid green, palm-like leaves made up of five leaflets. The snapdragon-like flowers are bright red with a yellow throat, and carried on erect spikes up to 6in (15cm) long. There are two good cultivars: *A. p.* 'Atrosanguinea', which has deeper red flowers, and *A. p.* 'Humilis', which has a low, spreading habit. *A. hippocastanum* is the common horse chestnut or conker tree. Propagation is by seed sown in spring, budding in summer or grafting indoors in spring (for named cultivars).

Amelanchier canadensis

Snowy mespilus
HEIGHT: 20ft (6m) • Hardy
FLOWERING SEASON: Late spring

This is a deciduous, suckering shrub or small tree with a dense, upright habit and dark whippy shoots. The oval, mid to dark green leaves with toothed margins are woolly when young, and turn vivid shades of yellow, orange and red in autumn. Brilliant white, star-shaped flowers, are carried in bold erect spikes in spring before the leaves have developed, followed by small, purple, currant-like fruits in late summer. Propagation is by seed sown in early autumn. Fireblight may cause shrivelling of young shoots and flowers.

Erysimum cheiri

Wallflower
HEIGHT: 2ft (60cm) • Hardy
FLOWERING SEASON: Spring

Evergreen shrubby perennial, with woody stems forming a low mound. The strap-like leaves are dark green and slightly paler on the underside. The flat, four-petalled flowers are carried above the leaves in dense spikes. Of several named cultivars the most popular is *E. c.* 'Harpur Crewe', with double, mustard-yellow, fragrant flowers; this lasts about five years. Propagation is by softwood cuttings taken in summer. Clubroot causes stunted top growth and death.

Exochorda × macrantha 'The Bride'

Pearl bush/Bride bush
HEIGHT: 5ft (1.5m) • Hardy
FLOWERING SEASON: Late spring/early summer

A deciduous, arching, free-flowering shrub that flourishes in sun. It likes loamy soil and should have a top dressing of farmyard compost every other year. It eventually forms a thick mound covered with large, attractively-shaped, white flowers in late spring. Pruning is not really necessary but the plant benefits from thinning the old shoots after flowering. Exochordas are spectacular enough to merit an isolated place in the garden. Propagation is by cuttings of young shoots taken in late summer.

Forsythia suspensa

Golden bell
HEIGHT: 8ft (2.5m) • Hardy
FLOWERING SEASON: Spring

These ubiquitous shrubs, with their open, spreading habit and long, gently arching, grey-brown branches are a familiar sight in spring. The light to mid green leaves which are roughly oval in shape, turn butter-yellow in autumn. Delicate, pale to golden yellow flowers are produced abundantly in spring on the previous year's growth before the leaves emerge. They should be pruned after flowering. Propagation is by hardwood cuttings taken in the winter.

Geranium 'Johnson's Blue'

Cranesbill
HEIGHT: 2½ft (75cm) • Hardy (most)
FLOWERING SEASON: Late spring

The leaves of many of these versatile herbaceous perennials are their main attraction. Deeply notched to form a palm-like shape, they are carried on tough, thin leaf stalks and in many varieties turn orange-scarlet in autumn. The flowers appear as large clusters of small, saucer-shaped blooms. There are a large number of geraniums and among the easiest to grow are: G. 'Johnson's Blue' and G. *endressii*. They prefer a sunny position in well-drained garden soil. Propagation is by division in early spring.

Geranium pratense

Meadow cranesbill
HEIGHT: 2ft (60cm) • Hardy
FLOWERING SEASON: Midsummer

This low-growing perennial is another popular member of the large genus of hardy cranesbills. It has mid green, deeply lobed leaves with a scalloped margin, held above the ground on thin green leaf stalks. The saucer-shaped flowers have five petals, and are violet-blue with clearly marked red veins on each petal. The cultivar 'Mrs Kendall Clark', is very free flowering, with clear blue flowers. Propagation is by division in early spring. In autumn the leaves of these plants turn orange before dying down for winter.

Gypsophila 'Rosenschleier' syn. 'Rosy Veil'

Baby's breath/Chalk plant
HEIGHT: 3ft (1m) • Hardy
FLOWERING SEASON: Summer

These cottage garden favourites have thin, strap-like, grey-green leaves very like those of the carnation, carried on thick, grey-green stems. Masses of very small flowers are produced in large clusters. Dwarf and pink-flowered cultivars are available as well as a double cultivar, G. *paniculata* 'Bristol Fairy'. G. *repens* 'Rosea' is very low-growing, 4-6in (10-15cm), and spreads to form a dense mat, with small, rose-pink flowers produced in abundance. Propagation is by root cuttings.

Hydrangea aspera
Villosa Group

Hydrangea
HEIGHT: 10ft (3m) • Hardy
FLOWERING SEASON: Late summer/autumn

The Villosa Group hydrangeas are rather
gaunt shrubs with narrow bluish green leaves
above and grey down underneath. In late
summer they carry large flower heads with a
mass of small purple-pink flowers in the
centre surrounded by larger pinkish-white
flowers on the outside. The whole effect is
most striking and attractive. They prefer
partial shade and moist soil. Propagation is
by softwood cuttings taken in summer.

Iris germanica

Common German flag
HEIGHT: 2½ft (75cm) • Hardy
FLOWERING SEASON: Spring/summer

This tough evergreen plant has dark green,
strap-like leaves up to 2ft (60cm) in length.
The primrose-scented flowers have silky
purple petals with a yellow centre. They are
carried on short stems in late spring. Among
many good hybrids are: I. 'Black Swan', with
deep, blue-black flowers with a dark blue
beard, and the free-flowering I. 'Wabash',
which has white standards and violet-blue
falls. Bearded irises of which this is one will
grow in most ordinary soils enriched by
compost. Propagation is by division of established plants immediately after flowering.

Juniperus virginiana
'Sulphur Spray'

Pencil cedar
HEIGHT: 21ft (7m) • Hardy
FLOWERING SEASON: Spring

These versatile hardy conifers come in a vast
array of cultivars. The low-growing, 'prostrate' cultivars make very good ground cover
for low maintenance gardens. In contrast,
J. scopulorum 'Skyrocket', with its silvery
blue-green foliage, is probably the most
narrow and upright conifer in cultivation.
The wood of *J. virginiana* was used to make
lead pencils. Propagation is by semi-ripe
cuttings with a heel taken in early autumn.

Kerria japonica 'Pleniflora'

Jew's mallow
HEIGHT: 10ft (3m) • Hardy
FLOWERING SEASON: Spring

A hardy leaf losing shrub with bright green
leaves and arching shoots with yellow, spiky,
pompom-type flowers carried on the
branches in spring. They are often grown
against a wall where they may have to be tied
back. Kerria is one of the easiest shrubs to
grow and tolerates all soil conditions but
does best in sun where the soil has been
deeply dug and enriched by compost or
manure. Mature plants form clumps and
propagation is by dividing the clumps in late
autumn.

Kolkwitzia amabilis

Beauty bush
HEIGHT: 10ft (3m) • Hardy
FLOWERING SEASON: Late spring/early summer

This medium-sized shrub is commonly
known as the beauty bush, a name it thoroughly deserves. The small, bell-shaped
flowers, which are a soft-pink with a trace
of yellow in the open throat, hang in small
clusters on the thin twiggy branches. The
light olive-green leaves are tinged red when
young. The thin, twiggy shoots are erect
when young but develop a drooping habit
as they become older. Prefers full sun and
fertile well-drained soil. Propagated from
semi-ripe cuttings taken in midsummer.

Lavatera 'Barnsley'

Tree mallow
HEIGHT: 6ft(1.8m) • Moderately hardy
FLOWERING SEASON: Summer/autumn

A popular vigorous garden plant which may
keep its leaves in mild winters, in the summer it carries a multitude of pinkish-white
flowers with a deeper pink circle at the
centre. The leaves are a greyish green.
L. 'Rosea' is bright pink. Lavateras must
have well-drained soil and do not do well in
heavy clay or soil that is very acidic. They
like a sunny position. Cut the whole plant
down to within 1ft (30cm) of the ground in
the spring. Propagate by semi-ripe cuttings
in summer or hardwood cuttings in winter.

Lonicera × *brownii* 'Dropmore Scarlet'

Scarlet trumpet honeysuckle
HEIGHT: 10ft (3m) • Hardy
FLOWERING SEASON: Mid/late summer

These attractive twining climbers have fragrant flowers which are tubular, opening out to a broad mouth, carried individually or in clusters. The colours range from white through pale yellow to gold, pink and scarlet. The pale to mid green leaves vary in shape from broadly oval to almost circular. *L. periclymenum* cultivars are very popular. Propagation is by semi-ripe cuttings taken in autumn.

Lupinus Russell Hybrids

Lupin
HEIGHT: 4ft (1.2m) • Hardy
FLOWERING SEASON: Summer

One of the delights of the herbaceous border in high summer, lupins are easy to grow and flourish in most soils. They prefer a sunny position. They come in a variety of colours which range from yellow to purple, blue and red. They are best raised from seed sown in the spring and planted out in position in the autumn, or they can be propagated by basal cuttings taken in the spring. The plants are not long-lived and will require replacing every 3 or 4 years. Prone to attack by aphids.

Morus nigra

Black mulberry
HEIGHT: 24ft (7.5m) • Hardy
FLOWERING SEASON: Early spring

This remarkable tree has large, grey-green pointed leaves, with a coarsely toothed margin and a coarse texture. The leaves give a striking display of autumn colour. The catkin-like flowers are of little significance and often go unnoticed, but are followed in autumn by reddish-purple, blackberry-like fruit, almost black when ripe, which is juicy and very tasty. Propagation is by hardwood cuttings taken in early winter and rooted out in the open ground.

Nigella damascena

Love-in-a-mist/Devil-in-a-bush
HEIGHT: 2ft (60cm) • Hardy
Flowering Season: Summer

A hardy annual grown for its attractive blue flowers, the flowers are set among very finely divided leaf stems which add considerably to their charms. *N. d.* 'Miss Jekyll' has darker blue flowers and *N. d.* 'Persian Jewels' has white, pink or blue flowers. The flowers are followed by decorative seed pods much used in flower arranging but if these are not required it is best to dead head the plant as this prolongs the flowering period. Likes sun and fertile well-drained soil. Sow seed in spring for flowers that summer.

Osmanthus delavayi

HEIGHT: 8ft (2.5m) • Hardy
FLOWERING SEASON: Spring

An evergreen shrub, *O. delavayi* is from China and was originally introduced in 1890. It has oval, toothed leaves which are a dark, glossy green. It produces clusters of small tubular white flowers which are highly fragrant. It will grow in sun or partial shade and prefers well-drained soil, but ideally needs a site sheltered from cold winds. The species, *O. heterophyllus*, makes a good hedging plant. If growing *O. heterophyllus* as a hedge, trim it regularly. To propagate take half-ripe cuttings in summer or layer branches in autumn.

Ostrya carpinifolia

Hop hornbeam
HEIGHT: 50ft (15m) • Hardy
FLOWERING SEASON: Mid spring

This attractive tree has greyish-purple bark on the main trunk and reddish-brown shoots which carry the glossy, dark green, oval leaves, which turn butter-yellow in the autumn. The flowers are long yellow catkins which hang from the bare branches in large quantities in spring. Green, hop-like fruits appear in autumn which later turn brown, they have a small nut-type seed under each 'hop' scale. For small gardens, the smaller *O. virginiana* is more useful. Propagation is by seed sown in late autumn or early spring.

Paeonia delavayi

Tree peony
HEIGHT: 6ft (1.8m) • Hardy
FLOWERING SEASON: Summer

The tree peony is a deciduous shrub with erect branches and an open suckering habit, the pale-brown bark flakes from the stems as they age. Large, oval leaves are finely divided into pointed sections with reddish-green stalks. The small, cup-shaped, single red flowers have golden stamens in the centre, and are followed by green, black-seeded fruits in autumn. Propagation is by seed sown in autumn or semi-ripe cuttings taken in summer.

Philadelphus coronarius 'Variegatus'

Mock orange
HEIGHT: 6ft (1.8m) • Hardy
FLOWERING SEASON: Summer

This deciduous, bushy shrub has a dense, upright habit and mid green, oval leaves. The small, creamy-white flowers are noted for their heady fragrance. A number of cultivars have coloured leaves: *P. c.* 'Aureus' has golden-yellow leaves, which turn lemon-green as they age, and *P. c.* 'Variegatus' green leaves edged with white. Propagation is by softwood cuttings taken in summer or hardwood cuttings taken in autumn and winter.

Phillyrea latifolia

HEIGHT: 10ft (3m) • Hardy
FLOWERING SEASON: Late spring/early summer

An evergreen shrub which has small but very fragrant flowers. The small, elliptical strap-like leaves are a shiny dark green and leathery. The small, scented white flowers are carried in clusters at the end of the young, branching stems. They are sometimes followed by blackcurrant-like fruits in autumn. Many of the branches tend to arch over so that a loose mound-like shrub is formed. It likes a sunny position and well-drained soil. Propagation is by semi-ripe cuttings taken in early summer.

Phlomis fruticosa

Jerusalem sage
HEIGHT: 3ft (1m) • Hardy
FLOWERING SEASON: Summer

An attractive, summer-flowering shrub, which forms a dense evergreen mound of straggly twiggy branches. The unusually shaped yellow flowers are produced in large ball-shaped trusses on the shoot tips. Broadly oval grey-green, coarsely textured leaves have a felty surface which turns slightly yellow in autumn. The young erect stems are also covered in felt, which disappears by the end of the first year of growth. Prune in late spring after the last frosts. Propagation is by softwood cuttings taken in late summer.

Populus alba 'Raket'

White poplar
HEIGHT: 80ft (25m) • Hardy
FLOWERING SEASON: Early spring

A deciduous tree with a broad, spreading habit, dark grey-green fissured bark, and young shoots which are covered with a thick white felt. The main attraction is the foliage: dark green leaves which have a silver down on the underside turn golden yellow in autumn. The cultivar *P. a.* 'Richardii' is much slower-growing and has small golden leaves which are white beneath. Poplar trees like coastal districts. Propagation is by hardwood cuttings taken in autumn. Silver leaf fungus kills large branches.

Potentilla fruticosa 'Hopley's Orange'

HEIGHT: 4ft (1.2m) • Hardy
FLOWERING SEASON: Spring/summer

This is a compact, bushy shrub with masses of spindly branches, with orange-brown bark which turns grey-brown and flakes with age. Deeply lobed, mid green leaves are in dense clusters over the younger branches. Flowers are small, buttercup-yellow and borne in clusters of no more than three blooms. Numerous named cultivars include the low-growing, *P. f.* 'Red Ace', with vermilion flowers and *P. f.* 'Abbotswood', with dark green foliage and white flowers. Propagation is by semi-ripe cuttings taken in autumn.

Prunus sargentii

Sargent cherry
HEIGHT: 25ft (8m) • Hardy
FLOWERING SEASON: Early/mid spring

This tree produces vast quantities of clear, single, shell-pink flowers in large clusters, which are complemented by the emerging glossy, bronze-red foliage of the new season's growth. Even more striking is the dramatic change of foliage colour in early autumn when the leaves turn yellow, orange and crimson shades before falling. Most ornamental cherries are propagated by budding or grafting in commercial nurseries, and offered for sale as young trees.

Robinia hispida

Rose acacia
HEIGHT: 6ft (1.8m) • Hardy
FLOWERING SEASON: Late spring/early summer

This attractive deciduous shrub has a loose, open habit and slightly arching branches, which are brittle and break very easily. The dark green leaves, which consist of up to thirteen small, oval leaflets arranged along a green central leaf stalk, turn butter-yellow in autumn. The large, sweet pea-like flowers are deep rose-pink, and are borne in long dangling clusters. It is ideal for training up against a wall or fence. The shrub tolerates most soils except for waterlogged sites and prefers full sun. Propagation is by seed sown in spring.

Romneya coulteri

Californian tree poppy
HEIGHT: 6ft (1.8m) • Moderately hardy
FLOWERING SEASON: Late summer

A striking and beautiful summer flowering perennial which needs the shelter of a south or south-west wall. It has large fragrant white flowers with prominent centres of golden-yellow stamens which appear in late summer. The leaves are deeply divided and grey-green in colour. It needs well-drained soil enriched by compost or leaf mould. Cut back the stems in the spring. Propagation is by root cuttings taken in the spring or by seed sown in the autumn.

Rosmarinus officinalis

Rosemary
HEIGHT: 6ft (1.8m) • Moderately hardy
FLOWERING SEASON: Spring/autumn

This popular aromatic shrub has an erect open habit, with narrow, aromatic, evergreen leaves that are mid to dark green in colour with pale green undersides. The tubular flowers, which range in colour from white to blues, pinks and mauves, are produced in small clusters at the leaf joints. These plants do not respond favourably to hard pruning, just trim back any straggling shoots. They grow best in well-drained soil and full sun. Propagation is by semi-ripe cuttings taken in late summer and early autumn.

Sambucus racemosa

Red-berried elder
HEIGHT: 9ft (3m) • Hardy
FLOWERING SEASON: Late spring

This is a large deciduous shrub with a broad, spreading habit. It is grown for its lush foliage and colourful fruits. The leaves are mid green and divided into five oval leaflets joined at the base to form a 'hand'. They turn pale yellow in autumn. In spring, large flat heads of white flowers are produced, to be followed by huge clusters of bright red berries in autumn. The cultivar *S. r.* 'Plumosa Aurea' has golden, finely-cut leaves. Elders grow almost anywhere. Propagation is by hardwood cuttings taken in winter.

Scabiosa 'Butterfly Blue'

Scabious
HEIGHT: 2ft (60cm) • Hardy
FLOWERING SEASON: Summer/autumn

A clump-forming herbaceous perennial with leaves that are divided into narrow segments. The large flowers, which range from white through blue to mauves and pinks, are borne on long, slender, leafless stems. *S. caucasica* 'Clive Greaves' is a rich mauve; 'Miss Willmott' is the best white cultivar. Two recent introductions are the more compact species 'Butterfly Blue' and 'Pink Mist'. It likes a sunny position and well-drained soil. Propagation is by softwood cuttings taken in spring and summer, or division in spring.

Spiraea betulifolia

Meadowsweet
HEIGHT: 3ft (1m) • Hardy
FLOWERING SEASON: Spring

Spiraeas are hardy deciduous shrubs grown for their leaf colour and the masses of small flowers that appear in spring and summer. *S.* 'Arguta' known as the 'Bridal wreath', has arched branches covered with white flowers in May as has *S. betulifolia*. *S. japonica* 'Goldflame' is a more upright arching shrub with orange-red young leaves in the spring and heads of deep rose-pink flowers. Spiraeas can be grown in most soils and semi-shade. Propagate by semi-ripe cuttings in summer.

Stachyurus chinensis

HEIGHT: 12ft (4m) • Hardy
FLOWERING SEASON: Winter

These winter-flowering shrubs do well on most soils and deserve to be more common than they are. When young, the plant has an upright habit, later forming a network of branching, purple-green shoots. The dark green, purple-tinged leaves are deeply veined, large, oval and end in a point. The small, pale yellow flowers, which are in long catkin-like structures, are borne freely along the bare branches in winter and spring. Propagation is by layering of low branches or semi-ripe cuttings taken in summer.

Symphoricarpos × *doorenbosii* 'Mother of Pearl'

Snowberry
HEIGHT: 5ft (1.5m) • Hardy
FLOWERING SEASON: Summer

The common snowberry, *S. albus* has small pink flowers in summer followed by white round berries which can be seen on bushes all winter as they are often ignored by the birds. *S.* × *d.* 'Mother of Pearl' has pink berries and *S. orbiculatus*, the coral berry, has white flowers and red berries. They can be grown in all soils and in shade as well as sun. They can make a useful informal hedge. Propagate by semi-ripe cuttings in summer.

Syringa × *henryi*

Lilac
HEIGHT: 5-15ft (1.5-4.5m) • Moderately hardy
FLOWERING SEASON: Summer

Attractive, deciduous shrubs, lilacs have mid green leaves, arranged along the twiggy branches in opposite pairs. The small flowers are carried in spikes at the tips of shoots, they are very fragrant, tubular and range in colour from deep pink through mauve to white. There are a number of species and cultivars available and care should be taken to select one that does not grow too large. They flourish in light or heavy fertile soil and prefer a sunny site. Propagation is by semi-ripe cuttings taken in mid to late summer.

Teucrium fruticans

Shrubby germander
Height: 6ft (1.8m) • Moderately hardy
Flowering Season: Summer

An evergreen shrub sometimes called the tree germander which has rather untidy pointing branches. These carry blue-grey silvery aromatic leaves which are white underneath. In the summer blue flowers appear along the length of each branch. It likes full sun and fertile well-drained soil and is a useful addition to any mixed border. It does not require pruning except to remove straggly branches and any dead wood in the spring. Propagate by semi-ripe cuttings taken in the summer.

Thuja occidentalis 'Sunkist'

Eastern white cedar
HEIGHT: 60ft (18m) • Hardy
FLOWERING SEASON: Early spring

This is a vigorous, long-lived tree with a neat conical shape. The bark, which is light to reddish-brown, peels and flakes off as the tree ages. The flat leaves are made up of many small, scale-like sections, and have a strong 'pineapple' aroma which is released when the leaves are crushed. The cones are small and brown. *T. plicata* 'Zebrina' has yellow bands on the leaves which are so close together that the plant appears to be golden. Propagation is by semi-ripe cuttings taken in spring or autumn.

Viburnum tinus

Verbascum chaixii

Mullein
HEIGHT: 3ft (1m) • Hardy
FLOWERING SEASON: Summer

This evergreen perennial has large, nettle-like leaves which are grey-green in colour and covered with a fine, grey felt. The slender spires of yellow flowers with purple centres are produced in mid- and late summer and the white-flowered cultivar *V. c.* 'Album', is even more striking. Propagation is by seed in spring or late summer or by root cuttings in winter. Aphids are often a problem but mullein moth caterpillars are possibly the most devastating pest.

Laurustinus
HEIGHT: 5ft (1.5m) • Hardy
FLOWERING SEASON: Winter

This evergreen shrub has an upright habit when young but becomes a rather open, round-topped, spreading plant as it ages. The broadly oval, dark green leaves have paler undersides and are arranged in pairs along the dark, greenish-brown stems which end in flat clusters of small, white, slightly fragrant tubular flowers. Possibly the best plant is *V. t.* 'Eve Price', which has flowers that are deep rose-pink in bud, opening to white flushed with pink. It tolerates most soils and some shade. Propagation is by semi-ripe cuttings taken in early summer.

Weigela florida 'Foliis Purpureis'

Bush honeysuckle
HEIGHT: 3ft (1m) Hardy
FLOWERING SEASON: Spring/early summer

A deciduous, low-growing, bushy shrub which has funnel-shaped flowers, bright pink on the outside and a paler pink shading to white within. The leaves are a dullish dark green. Weigelas will grow in almost any soil and while they prefer sun they will tolerate some shade. Prune established plants after flowering by cutting out up to one third of the branches to ground level. Propagate by semi-ripe cuttings in summer.

More Plants for Alkaline Soil

Many plants can be grown on chalk (alkaline) soil. The list is very large and we can only give a small selection of the most suitable plants but it should be noted that most bulbs do well on chalk (limestone).

Gardening on chalk (limestone) is governed by the depth of soil over the under-lying chalk (alkaline) or limestone strata, chalk soil is inclined to be dry and hungry. It can be improved by adding copious quantities of farmyard manure, leaf mould, garden compost (soil mix) and turf and the fertility can be improved by adding dried blood and balanced artificial fertilisers.

TREES
Abies koreana
Acer (in variety)
Betula (in variety)
Carpinus betulus
Catalpa bignonioides
Cercidiphyllum japonicum
Chimonanthus praecox
Corylus (in variety)
Crataegus (in variety)
Davidia involucrata
Fagus (in variety)
Ficus carica
Fraxinus angustifolia

Koelreuteria paniculata
Larix decidua
Liquidambar styraciflua 'Worplesdon'
Malus (in variety)
Pyrus (in variety)
Sorbus (in variety)

SHRUBS
Aronia arbutifolia
Artemesia absinthium
Berberis (in variety)
Buddleja (in variety)
Chaenomeles japonica
Choisya ternata
Cornus (in variety)
Cotinus coggygria
Escallonia (in variety)
Euonymus fortunei cvs.
Jasminum officinale
Lavandula (in variety)
Ligustrum ovalifolium
Mahonia (in variety)
Myrtus communis
Osmanthus (in variety)
Philadelphus (in variety)
Ribes laurifolium
R. 'Königin von Dänemark'
R. 'Madame Legras de Saint Germain'
(Old-fashioned and Alba roses are particularly suitable for poor soil and conditions)
Rosmarinus officinalis
Salvia officinalis
Sarcococca hookeriana
Senecio (*Brachyglottis*) 'Sunshine'

Stepanandra tanakae
Syringa (in variety)
Viburnum (in variety)

PERENNIALS & GROUND COVER PLANTS
Alchemilla mollis
Amenone × hybrida
Aruncus dioicus
Aster novi-belgii
Astilbe (in variety)
Bergenia (in variety)
Campanula carpatica
Catananche caerulea
Ceratostigma willmottianum
Crambe cordifolia
Dianthus (in variety)
Dicentra (in variety)
Digitalis (in variety)
Echinops bannaticus
Geranium (in variety)
Helianthemum (in variety)
Iris (in variety)
Lamium maculatum
Leucanthemum × superbum
Nepeta × faassenii
Penstemon (in variety)
Perovskia atriplicifolia
Phlox paniculata
Polygonatum × hybridum
Primula auricula 'Adrian'
Pulmonaria saccharata
Santolina chamaecyparissus
Veronica prostrata
Vinca (in variety)

PLANTS
for CLAY SOILS

Although part of the garden landscape in many areas, clay soil can be difficult to deal with, becoming waterlogged in winter and baked hard in summer. Plants suffer alternately from too much water or from drought. Here is a selection of plants that is attractive and tough enough to cope with these far from ideal conditions.

ABOVE: Houttuynia cordata *'Chameleon', a robust ground-covering perennial with lovely leaf colour that likes moisture and appreciates some sun. It grows well beside water.*

OPPOSITE: *Foxgloves make an impressive bank at the back of a border with yellow hemerocallis, geranium and lady's mantle at the front.*

ABOVE: *Big clump-forming hostas, such as* Hosta crispula *with its wavy-edged, cream-splashed leaves, are successful on clay, as are the drifts of* Persicaria bistorta, *with its spires of pink flowers in summer.*

Clay is one of those substances that is wonderful in small quantities, but a real nuisance if you have too much of it. It is an essential part of a good soil, because it holds onto the nutrients that plants need for healthy growth, and retains moisture, so that plants growing in it suffer less from drought in all but the driest of summers. Unfortunately, despite these advantages, really heavy, wet, sticky clay soil is often totally unworkable, and it is also cold in spring, which can quickly rot delicate plants.

These difficulties come about as a direct result of the composition of the soil. The particles that make up a clay soil are the smallest found in mineral soils, with the result that the water retained in the tiny spaces between the particles binds them together into an unresponsive mass. Physically working this soil is largely a matter of timing; try to do it when it is too wet and it will smear and form a 'pan' at the depth you go down to, forming an impenetrable layer for plant roots and draining water alike. Leave it until it is too dry, on the other hand, and you are working with what feels like lumps of rock. Once you have experienced both situations, it will become apparent that you must establish the ideal state in which to tackle your soil.

Clay soils have a tendency to either become sticky and greasy when they are wet, or to bake hard and crack open when they dry out. This cracking process leaves deep crevices which speed up the drying-out process by exposing a greater surface area from which the moisture can evaporate. Any rain which falls then simply runs off without soaking in. At this stage, you would expect the plants to wilt and die, but even though the soil seems to be rock hard, enough water is still being held by the soil particles to sustain the plants for a while.

While water retention is a distinct advantage in summer, it is usually just the opposite in winter. So much water may be retained in the soil, and for such long periods, that plant roots have to be able to tolerate very damp conditions, often with little air to help compensate. Many members of the rose family thrive in these conditions; and aronia, chaenomeles (quince), cotoneaster, crataegus (hawthorn), malus (crab apple) and pyracantha do particularly well.

If the soil can be improved to make it more workable by the addition of organic matter to loosen it up, it will retain plant nutrients for longer periods than other soils, so that plants are able to use more of them before they are leached away by rain. Fertiliser applications are then more effective and the nutrients released by organic matter as it rots are used more effectively.

Finally, clay soils can be acid, neutral or alkaline, which will also affect your choice of plants, so a soil test is helpful if the vegetation in the immediate surroundings fails to give any clues. Although clay soils are more stable in their acidity and alkalinity, they are much more difficult to change. More often than not the limiting factor as to what you can grow on a clay soil will in fact be the soil pH reading rather than the clay content of your soil.

There are many bulbs, herbaceous perennials and marginal plants such as aruncus, lysimachia, mimulus, and tradescantia which prefer the cool, moist conditions that clay soils offer. As with any situation where one condition overrides the others, once you have chosen the plants which thrive under those circumstances, you can have as good a display as anywhere else. Grow plants with a vigorous constitution as those are the ones likely to do best.

BELOW: Persicaria bistorta, *at the front of the border, with iris,* Geranium phaeum *and* philadelphus *behind are all plants that will flourish in heavy soil. Roses are particularly suitable plants to grow if you garden on clay.*

Abelia × *grandiflora*

HEIGHT: 5ft (1.5m) • Hardy

FLOWERING SEASON: Late summer/late autumn

This hybrid shrub has glossy green, oval leaves carried on thin branches, giving the plant a loose, spreading appearance. The tubular flowers, borne in open clusters on the shoot tips, are slightly fragrant and a soft pink, which fades to white with age. Regular pruning is not required. It likes well-drained soil and a sheltered sunny position, some protection may be necessary in severe winters. This plant is easy to propagate from 4in (10cm) tip cuttings placed in a cold frame in late summer.

Acer platanoides

Norway maple

HEIGHT: 100ft (30m) • Hardy

FLOWERING SEASON: Spring

This is a vigorous tree with typical, palmate maple leaves. Bright green in summer, they turn a bright golden-yellow in the autumn. In the spring bright golden flowers are produced in broad flat clusters on the branches before the leaves. Two good cultivars are the purple-leaved *A. p.* 'Crimson King' and *A. p.* 'Drummondii', which has mid green leaves with a creamy-white margin. Propagation is by seed sown in the spring or, for named cultivars, budding in the summer.

Alcea rosea Chater's Double Group

Hollyhock

HEIGHT: 8ft (2.5m) • Hardy

FLOWERING SEASON: Summer

Hollyhocks are hardy biennial plants although in some cases they are short lived perennials. They are a familiar sight throughout cottage gardens and their large upright flower spikes make a focal point in any border. They should be raised from seed sown in a prepared bed in late spring and planted out in position in mid-autumn. Hollyhocks like well-drained soil and a sunny position. Rust may be a problem.

Alnus incana

Grey alder

HEIGHT: 60ft (18m) • Hardy

FLOWERING SEASON: Early spring

This is a deciduous tree with reddish-brown shoots and a wide conical habit. The broadly oval leaves are dark green on the upper surface, grey beneath and deeply veined, with slightly puckered margins. In late winter and early spring, dangling yellow catkins are produced close to the shoot tips. Alders grow in most conditions and this tree is ideal for poor soils and cold exposed sites. There is a golden-leafed cultivar *A. i.* 'Aurea'. Propagation is by seed sown in spring, or, for named cultivars, grafting.

Amaranthus caudatus

Love-lies-bleeding/Joseph's coat

HEIGHT: 3-4ft (1-1.2m) • Half-hardy

FLOWERING SEASON: Summer/autumn

This popular plant has broadly oval, light green leaves and crimson drooping, rope-like flowers up to 18in (45cm) long. The stems of the plant often turn crimson in the autumn. *A. c.* 'Viridis' has attractive pale green tassels, while a very striking variety, *A. tricolor* var. *salicifolius* is grown for its drooping, willow-like leaves which are shades of orange, reddish-pink and bronze. This easy-going plant will grow in any light, from full sun through to partial shade. Propagation is by seeds sown in early spring.

Anemone × *hybrida* 'Königin Charlotte'

Japanese anemone

HEIGHT: 3ft (1m) • Hardy

FLOWERING SEASON: Late summer/early autumn

This vigorous branching plant thrives in moist soils, in a partially shaded situation. The mid to deep green leaves are deeply cut and almost trifoliate. The shallowly cup-shaped flowers, which range from white to deep rose-pink with a bright core of yellow stamens, are carried on tall, thin, green stems. Among the cultivars are *A.* × *h.* 'Honorine Jobert' with white flowers, and the semi-double-flowered *A. hupehensis* var. *japonica* 'Bressingham Glow' with rosy-red blooms.

Aralia elata

Japanese angelica tree
HEIGHT: 25ft (8m) ◆ Hardy
FLOWERING SEASON: Late summer

This large suckering shrub has sparse, angular branches clad with short, broad-based prickles. It is grown for the beauty of its large clusters of dark green leaves which are arranged in a whorl on the end of each branch. Large spikes of small white flowers are carried on the tip of each branch from late August. A very attractive cultivar, *A.e.* 'Aureovariegata', has irregular, golden-yellow edged leaves. Propagate by root cuttings taken in late winter.

Aronia arbutifolia

Chokeberry
HEIGHT: 8ft (2.5m) ◆ Hardy
FLOWERING SEASON: Spring

A colourful, deciduous shrub which has a rather erect habit when young, but becomes lax and spreading with age. It is grown for its flowers, fruits and autumn colour. The leaves are narrowly oval, dark green with a grey-green underside, and turn shades of brilliant orange, crimson and purple in autumn. In spring, small, white, hawthorn-like flowers are produced in flat clusters, followed by small red berries. It prefers sun or semi-shade and moist well-drained soil. Propagation is by semi-ripe cuttings in summer or seed sown in spring.

Aruncus dioicus

Goat's beard
HEIGHT: 5ft (1.5m) ◆ Hardy
FLOWERING SEASON: Summer

This hummock-forming perennial has large, light green, deeply-veined leaves which are made up of several strap-like leaflets, held on tough sturdy stems. In the summer, large feathery plumes of creamy-white flowers are carried on strong thin reddish-green stems. In the autumn the female plants bear chestnut brown seed-heads, but it is the male plants that produce the best flowers. It will grow in any well-drained soil and likes full sun. Propagation is by division in winter.

Astilbe × arendsii

Goat's beard
HEIGHT: 3ft (1m) ◆ Hardy
FLOWERING SEASON: Midsummer

This hardy herbaceous perennial has deep green, finely cut, fern-like foliage, carried on thin wiry reddish-green stems; some of the red-flowered cultivars have bronze-green foliage in the spring. In the summer large, pointed spikes of plume-like blooms appear. A large number of cultivars are now available: *A.* 'Bressingham Beauty' has spikes of rich pink flowers, and *A.* 'Feuer', has salmon-red blooms. They like moist rich soil and at least partial shade. Propagation is by division in the winter.

Berberis × stenophylla

Barberry
HEIGHT: 8ft (2.5m) ◆ Hardy
FLOWERING SEASON: Late spring

This evergreen shrub has gracefully arching, slender branches, with small, orange-yellow flowers, which are followed by small, blue fruits. The small, glossy, dark green leaves are narrow and tipped with sharp spines. It is effective as an impenetrable, informal hedge, but also as an individual specimen plant. The dwarf cultivar *B. × s.* 'Crawley Gem', has a low, bushy habit and orange flowers which are red when in bud. They are soil tolerant and grow in sun or semi-shade. Propagation is by semi-ripe cuttings taken in summer.

Campsis radicans

Trumpet flower/Trumpet vine
HEIGHT: 30ft (9m) ◆ Moderately hardy
FLOWERING SEASON: Late summer/early autumn

A fast-growing plant ideal for sunny walls and fences, pergolas and gazebos, or other, similar structures. Four to twelve trumpet-like orange/red flowers are carried in clusters on the shoot tips. There are also red- and yellow-flowered cultivars. The light to mid green foliage consists of oval leaflets which form pinnate leaves. Good yellow autumn colour. Fast rate of growth. Likes sun and fertile, well-drained soil, water in the summer in dry spells. Propagation is by root cuttings taken in early spring.

Cardamine pratensis 'Flore Pleno'

Cuckoo flower/Lady's smock/Bitter cress
HEIGHT: 18in (45cm) • Hardy
FLOWERING SEASON: Late spring

This neat, clump-forming plant has mid green leaves divided into many small, rounded leaflets arranged in neat basal rosettes. *C. p.* 'Flore Pleno', produces loose, open clusters of double lilac flowers in late spring. This plant does not produce seed but is very easy to propagate: leaves in contact with a moist surface produce adventitious roots, and later shoots which can be divided up to produce more plants.

Celastrus orbiculatus

Oriental bittersweet/Staff vine
HEIGHT: 22ft (7m) • Hardy
FLOWERING SEASON: Summer

A large, vigorous, useful climber with oval, mid green leaves on short stalks and tiny greenish flowers carried on the female plant in summer. The leaves turn a good yellow in autumn. The twining stems are light grey-green, changing to light creamy-brown with age in early summer, followed by bright orange capsules containing a scarlet-coated seed if a male plant is available as a pollinator. Prefers shade and grows in most soils. Propagation is from seed sown in autumn.

Chaenomeles japonica

Japonica/Japanese quince
HEIGHT: 4ft (1.2m) • Hardy
FLOWERING SEASON: Spring

A colourful, slow-growing shrub with a lax spreading habit. The single flowers, orange-red with a golden centre, are produced in profusion along the older wood in spring, followed by bright yellow quince fruits. Elliptical leaves are green, changing to pale yellow in autumn. Often grown on walls it prefers sun and well-drained soil. Prune after flowering. Propagation is by semi-ripe cuttings taken with a heel in late summer. Coral spot fungus can cause problems.

Crambe cordifolia

Ornamental sea kale
HEIGHT: 6ft (1.8m) • Hardy
FLOWERING SEASON: Summer

A large spreading plant which forms a great clump when established and in the summer is covered with masses of small white fragrant flowers rather like a giant gypsophila. They are carried above large dark green crinkled leaves. *C. maritima* is a smaller plant more generally found in the kitchen garden where it can be grown as a spring vegetable. Kale is easy to cultivate in ordinary well-drained garden soil and tolerates some shade. Propagate by dividing up the clumps in the spring.

Darmera peltata

Umbrella plant
HEIGHT: 4ft (1.2m) • Hardy
FLOWERING SEASON: Spring

This is a spreading perennial with large, disc-like leaves which turn an interesting bronze-pink in the autumn. The pale pink flowers, which have a white reverse to the petals, are carried in large round clusters on dark greenish-brown stems, which are covered in fine white hairs. The flowers and stems appear before the leaves. It needs moist conditions and makes a fine water plant beside a pool. Grows in sun or shade. Propagation is by division of the rhizomes in spring or by seed in autumn.

Digitalis grandiflora

Foxglove
HEIGHT: 3ft (1m) • Hardy
FLOWERING SEASON: Late summer

This superb perennial foxglove forms a clump of strap-like leaves which are mid green and covered with soft hairs particularly on the underside. The clear, pale yellow flowers have a pattern of brown, net-like markings on the inside, and are carried on tall flower spikes up to 3ft (1m) or more in height. Foxgloves grow best in moist well-drained soil and semi-shade. This plant is relatively short-lived and must be replaced every third or fourth year. Propagation is by seed sown in late spring or early summer.

Dodecatheon pulchellum

Shooting star/American cowslip
HEIGHT: 18in (45cm) • Hardy
FLOWERING SEASON: Early summer

These clump-forming hardy herbaceous perennials have light green, elliptical leaves arranged in flat, spreading rosettes growing close to the ground. In the summer the nodding flowers appear on strong slender stems, each bloom is a circle of rose-purple petals which are swept back away from the bright yellow anthers in the centre of the flower. They prefer a shady position in moist soil. Propagation is by seed sown in autumn, or by division in winter.

Filipendula palmata 'Alba'

Meadowsweet/Dropwort
HEIGHT: 3ft (1m) • Hardy
FLOWERING SEASON: Midsummer

This attractive perennial has mid green, deeply cut foliage, giving the leaves a fern-like appearance. There is a double-flowered cultivar *F. vulgaris* 'Multiplex' which produces large spikes of creamy-white, plumes of flowers in summer which remain attractive for a long period. They grow best in a cool, moist situation with partial shade, and do not like too much disturbance. *F. rubra* has pink flowers and will grow in boggy ground. Propagation is by division in the winter.

Ginkgo biloba

Maidenhair tree
HEIGHT: 70ft (21m) • Hardy
FLOWERING SEASON: Spring

A most interesting and ornamental deciduous tree it has peculiarly shaped leaves with crinkled edges. They turn brilliant yellow and gold before falling in the autumn. The tree also carries fruits in the autumn, but it requires both male and female trees to be grown together for the flowers to become fertile. It prefers well-drained soil and tolerates some shade. The tree has been found in fossil beds millions of years old. It was often planted near temples.

Hemerocallis 'Burning Daylight'

Day lily
HEIGHT: 3ft (1m) • Hardy
FLOWERING SEASON: Summer

These are colourful, clump-forming plants, with leaves that are pale to mid green, strap-shaped, ending in a point at the tip. The brightly coloured, lily-like flowers only last for a day, but are produced in such abundance that this is hardly noticeable. The popular Kwanso cultivars include the orange, double-flowered *H. fulva* 'Flore Pleno' and the variegated *H. f.* 'Kwanso Variegata'. They like full sun and moist soil. Propagation is by division in early spring.

Hosta 'Spinners'

Plantain lily
HEIGHT: 2ft (60cm) • Hardy
FLOWERING SEASON: Late summer/early autumn

These hardy herbaceous perennials are grown for their attractive foliage. Leaf shapes range from long and narrow to oval with a pointed tip. Leaf colours can vary from blue to rich combinations of silver or golden variegations. The flowers are carried on spikes above the leaves. *H. sieboldiana* var. *elegans* has broadly spear-shaped, glossy, bluish-green leaves with prominent veins, and soft lilac-blue flowers. Propagation is by division in early spring, but replant immediately. The leaves are very prone to slug and snail damage.

Houttuynia cordata 'Chameleon'

HEIGHT: 18in (45cm) • Hardy
FLOWERING SEASON: Spring

This is a vigorous, spreading perennial with dark blue-green, aromatic, heart-shaped leaves, carried on reddish-green leaf stalks, and fleshy erect stems. This plant spreads rapidly by means of underground runners just below the soil surface. The white flowers are carried on the tips of erect stems just above the leaves. There is a double white cultivar *H. c.* 'Flore Pleno'. *H. c.* 'Chameleon' has leaves splashed with yellow and red on a dark green base. Propagation is by division in late autumn or early spring.

Humulus lupulus 'Aureus'

Golden hop
HEIGHT: 25ft (8m) • Hardy
FLOWERING SEASON: Late summer

An attractive self-supporting, perennial climber with thin bristly twining stems. The bristly leaves are toothed around the margins and are deeply lobed. The flowers are insignificant, but the fruit clusters are quite attractive in the autumn. *H. l.* 'Aureus' has soft, golden-yellow leaves, stems and fruits. There is a less vigorous variegated sort with creamy-white and green variegated leaves. Propagation is by semi-ripe cuttings taken in early and mid-summer.

Iris pseudacorus

Yellow flag
HEIGHT: 3ft (1m) • Hardy
FLOWERING SEASON: Spring/summer

This popular hardy herbaceous perennial known as yellow flag has buttercup yellow flowers and broad, strap-like, bluish-green foliage arranged in a fan. A very striking plant is *I. p.* 'Variegata', with its gold and green striped foliage. It will grow in a range of conditions but it really thrives in semi-shade, heavy soil and waterlogged conditions, and even in water up to 18in (45cm) deep. Propagation is by division immediately after the plant has flowered.

Lathyrus grandiflorus

Everlasting pea
HEIGHT: 10ft (3m) • Hardy
FLOWERING SEASON: Summer/autumn

Originally from Italy, this tall, self-supporting climber has curling tendrils at the tip of each of the mid green leaflets. The flowers are scented (especially in the evening) and come in a variety of colours, with pink, white and deep purple being the most popular. The cultivar *L. latifolius* 'White Pearl' gives a lovely cottage garden effect. Propagation is by seed sown in early autumn or early spring. Harden off before planting out. New growth is very prone to slug damage in wet seasons.

Leucanthemum × *superbum*

Shasta daisy
HEIGHT: 3ft (1m) • Hardy
FLOWERING SEASON: Mid/late summer

Formerly known as *Chrysanthemum* × *superbum* this is a valued perennial, with strap-shaped, dark green leaves. The single flowers are white with a golden centre, carried on tall green stems. The species is rarely grown, as cultivars with improved flowers have been introduced. These include *L.* × *s.* 'Snowcap', with a dwarfing habit and white daisy-like flowers, and *L.* × *s.* 'Wirral Supreme', with large double flowers with a golden centre. Propagation is by division in winter or by basal cuttings taken in spring.

Mimulus × *burnetii*

Musk/Monkey flower
HEIGHT: 12in (30cm) • Hardy
FLOWERING SEASON: Early/late summer

This low, spreading plant thrives in cool, damp soil, but likes to have its head in the sunshine. They can be good plants for the bog garden and waterside. The elliptical, mid green leaves are carried on square stems and often have a green bract-like leaf at the point where the leaf stalk is attached to the stem. Yellow, snapdragon-like flowers open to reveal a throat mottled with brown and purple markings. Propagation is by division in the spring or seed sown in the autumn or spring, but it will often layer itself in wet soil.

Myosotis scorpioides

Water forget-me-not
HEIGHT: 10in (25cm) • Hardy
FLOWERING SEASON: Late spring/midsummer

This is a moisture-loving evergreen perennial with a long flowering period in summer when it produces branching green stems of minute blue flowers with a yellow-orange 'eye'. Spoon-shaped leaves are carried on thin green stems and covered with fine hairs when young. It is often grown as a marginal water plant. A cultivar with larger flowers is *M. s.* 'Mermaid', which has a sprawling habit and forms a loose mound. These plants last only for three or four years. Propagate by semi-ripe basal cuttings taken in spring.

Persicaria bistorta 'Superba'

Knotweed/Snakeweed
HEIGHT: 4ft (1.2m) • Hardy
FLOWERING SEASON: Summer

Persicarias were formerly known as
polygonums and have the common name of
knotweed. *P .b.* 'Superba' which is sometimes called snakeweed, can be invasive, but
makes an attractive drift beside a water feature. It forms large clumps of arrow-shaped,
centrally ribbed, mid green leaves and spires
of soft pink flowers throughout the summer.
It will cope with sun or partial shade, but
needs moist soil. Propagate by division in
spring or autumn or raise from seed.

Phlox paniculata 'Fujiyama'

HEIGHT: 3ft (1m) • Hardy
FLOWERING SEASON: Late summer

Colourful upright perennials *P. paniculata*
cultivars have tubular, five-lobed flowers,
generally pink in colour, carried on conical heads: among the best known are
'Amethyst', violet, 'Norah Leigh', pale
lilac, and 'Franz Schubert', pink. They like
deep rich soil that does not dry out, and
semi-shade. Cut down to soil level after
flowering and propagate by division in
spring or semi-ripe cuttings in summer.

Phormium tenax

New Zealand flax
HEIGHT: 4ft (1.2m) • Moderately hardy
FLOWERING SEASON: Summer

This clump-forming, evergreen perennial
has bold, sword-shaped leaves which have a
tough, leathery texture and are deep green
in colour. When the plant has established,
dull orange flowers are borne on large, erect
spikes. These are followed by scimitar-
shaped seed capsules. Among the cultivars
with variegated foliage, *P.* 'Dazzler' has
leaves with shades of yellow, salmon-pink,
orange-red and bronze. Propagation is by
seed sown in the spring or division in spring.

Populus × *candicans* 'Aurora'

Ontario poplar/Balm of Gilead
HEIGHT: 80ft (25m) • Hardy
FLOWERING SEASON: Spring

A large tree with a broad crown and broad,
almost heart-shaped, leaves which have a
strong scent of balsam in the spring. The
attractive *P.* × *c.* 'Aurora' has variegated foliage, the dark green leaves being splashed with
pale green, creamy-white and pink. It must be
pruned very hard each spring to maintain this
striking effect. Poplars prefers full sun and
deep moist well-drained soil. They have
extensive root systems and are not suitable
for planting close to buildings. Propagation
is by hardwood cuttings taken in autumn.

Pterocarya fraxinifolia

Caucasian wing nut
HEIGHT: 80ft (25m) • Hardy
FLOWERING SEASON: Summer

A moisture-loving, spreading, deciduous tree,
with a characteristic short trunk and deeply
grooved bark. The glossy, dark green ash-like
leaves are made up of many finely toothed
leaflets and turn yellow in autumn. The
flowers consist of long green catkins up to
18in (45cm) long, which are followed by
greenish-brown winged fruits in autumn. It
likes a sunny position and moist well-drained
soil. Propagation is by softwood cuttings in
summer, by seed sown outdoors in spring or
by removing the suckers.

Pyracantha 'Orange Glow'

Firethorn
HEIGHT: 10ft (3m) • Hardy
FLOWERING SEASON: Early summer

Versatile evergreen shrubs, with attractive
foliage, fruit and flowers, these are useful for
hedging, as wall shrubs or free-standing
specimens. The large clusters of small white,
or pale pink blooms are followed by clusters
of round fruits in autumn, coloured yellow,
orange or red depending upon the cultivar.
Oval, glossy, dark evergreen leaves with a
finely toothed margin, are carried on brown
stems with sharp spines. Propagation is by
semi-ripe cuttings taken in summer. Pyracantha scab may cause premature leaf drop.

Pyrus calleryana

Callery pear
HEIGHT: 50ft (15m) • Hardy
FLOWERING SEASON: Mid/late spring

This is a medium-sized, deciduous tree with a broadly conical habit and slightly erect thorny branches. The glossy green leaves are broadly oval. Clusters of single white, cup-shaped flowers are produced in spring, and are followed by small brown fruits in autumn. The cultivar *P. c.* 'Chanticleer' has a narrow conical habit and is particularly attractive in autumn when the leaves turn a reddish-purple. Propagation is by budding in summer or by grafting in winter.

Quercus palustris

Pin oak
HEIGHT: 50ft (15m) • Hardy
FLOWERING SEASON: Late spring/early summer

A fast-growing, dense-headed, deciduous tree with a spreading habit and slender branches that droop gracefully at the tips. As this tree ages, the bark becomes purplish-grey and deeply grooved. The leaves, which are a shining dark green on the upper surface and pale green below, have deeply lobed margins, turn a rich scarlet in autumn. The small flowers are produced in late spring, and greenish-brown 'acorns' follow in autumn. Propagation is by seed sown outdoors in spring.

Rheum palmatum

Rhubarb
HEIGHT: 6ft (1.8m) • Hardy
FLOWERING SEASON: Summer

Most ornamental rhubarbs have large, glossy, mid green leaves which are held above the crown on thick fleshy stalks. The small flowers are carried above the leaves on tall spikes. *R. alexandrae* is grown for its 3ft (1m) flower spikes. These have large papery bracts like drooping tongues covering the small, inconspicuous flowers. *R. palmatum* has deeply cut, hand-shaped leaves and greenish-yellow flowers. They prefer moist conditions. Propagation is by division in winter.

Rodgersia pinnata 'Superba'

HEIGHT: 3ft (1m) • Moderately hardy
FLOWERING SEASON: Summer

This clump-forming herbaceous perennial is usually grown for its foliage. The deeply-veined leaves are made up of as many as nine deep green leaflets joined together by a thin, green, central leaf stalk. In the summer plumes of small pinkish-red, star-like flowers are produced on erect, bare, multi-branched stalks. The bronze-leaved *R. p.* 'Superba', is very good for autumn colour. It prefers some shade and a sheltered site but will grow in sun as long as the soil does not dry out. Propagation is by division of the rhizomes in spring.

Salix babylonica var. pekinensis 'Tortuosa'

Dragon's claw willow
HEIGHT: 50ft (15m) • Hardy
FLOWERING SEASON: Spring

This large shrub or small tree has unusual, corkscrew-shaped branches and green winter bark. A vigorous plant, initially it has a narrow shape, but spreads from the centre with age. The bright green leaves are narrow and strap-like, and may be quite straight or as twisted and contorted as the branches, with some leaves being curled up like a watch spring. Propagation is by hardwood cuttings, taken in late autumn and early winter when the plant is dormant.

Salix caprea

Goat willow/Pussy willow
HEIGHT: 30ft (9m) • Hardy
FLOWERING SEASON: Spring

This familiar large shrub or small tree is most noticeable in spring when male trees produce large, yellow catkins later becoming soft, silvery-grey 'pussy-willow' catkins. The fluffy seeds shed in early summer. The elliptical leaves are dark green on the upper surface and grey-green and hairy on the underside. As the shrub ages the grey-brown bark becomes deeply fissured. Propagation is by hardwood cuttings taken in winter and planted outside. The disease anthracnose often causes brown spots on leaves and stem die-back.

Sorbaria aitchisonii

HEIGHT: 9ft (3m) • Hardy

FLOWERING SEASON: Late summer

This very hardy, deciduous shrub makes a broad dome shape, with reddish-brown shoots and long spreading branches. The fern-like, mid green leaves are made up of many small leaflets, evenly arranged along a slender leaf stalk. In autumn the leaves turn golden-yellow and orange. Small, creamy-white blooms are produced in large flower spikes in late summer. Prefers sun and deep moist soil. This plant can be very invasive. Propagation is by semi-ripe cuttings with a heel taken in summer.

Tradescantia × andersoniana 'Purple Dome'

Spiderwort/Flower-of-a-day

HEIGHT: 2ft (60cm) • Hardy

FLOWERING SEASON: Summer/autumn

This herbaceous perennial is a popular plant for the mixed border, as it requires little care and flowers throughout the summer. It is attractive with dull green, strap-like leaves which taper to a narrow point. The flowers consist of three petals and are produced in small clusters. Among the hybrids are 'Blue Stone', with deep blue flowers, and 'Isis', with rich purple ones. Propagate by division in early or mid-spring.

Viburnum opulus

Guelder rose

HEIGHT: 15ft (4.5m) • Hardy

FLOWERING SEASON: Mid/late summer

A large deciduous popular shrub which has a vigorous, spreading habit. The dark green, sycamore-like leaves, which are carried on reddish-green leaf stalks, turn orange and yellow in autumn. The large, white, elder-like flowers are followed by translucent red berries. Striking cultivars include *V. o.* 'Xanthocarpum', which has all the characteristics of the type but golden-yellow berries, and the golden-leaved *V. o.* 'Aureum'.

More Plants for Clay Soil

Gardening on very heavy clay can be extremely difficult. If the sub-soil is moderately porous then, through cultivation, clay can usually be transformed into good garden soil on which most plants can be grown. If the sub-soil is incapable of carrying away water then the list of trees and plants that will survive is limited. To improve heavy clay the land should first be drained and then it should be dug roughly and the soil allowed to lie in clumps over winter. Don't attempt to cultivate the soil in wet periods and dig in grit, ashes and leaf mould when planting. Choose plants that have a vigorous constitution and which can look after themselves. Roses do particularly well on clay soil. Bulbs can be grown but they may not do so well if the soil becomes waterlogged.

TREES

Acer (in variety)
Amelanchier canadensis
Arbutus × andrachnoides
Betula ermanii
Catalpa bignonioides

Cercidiphyllum japonicum
Chimonanthus praecox,
Corylus avellana 'Contorta'
Crataegus (in variety)
Ficus carica
Fraxinus angustifolia
Liquidambar styraciflua
Malus (in variety)
Pyrus (in variety)
Sambucus racemosa
Taxodium distichum

SHRUBS

Artemesia absinthium
Berberis (in variety)
Chaenomeles (in variety)
Choisya ternata
Cornus (in variety)
Cotinus coggygria
Exochorda × macrantha 'The Bride'
Forsythia suspensa
Lavandula (in variety)
Lavatera 'Barnsley'
Ligustrum ovalifolium
Mahonia (in variety)
Philadelphus (in variety)
Roses
Salvia officinalis
Santolina chamaecyparissus
Sarcococca hookeriana
Stepanandra tanakae
Syringa (in variety)
Viburnum (in variety)

PERENNIALS & GROUND COVER PLANTS

Alchemilla mollis
Amenone × hybrida
Aquilegia alpina
Aster novi-belgii
Astrantia major
Aucuba japonica
Bergenia (in variety)
Buddleja (in variety)
Campanula carpatica
Centhranthus ruber
Dianthus (in variety)
Dicentra (in variety)
Digitalis (in variety)
Echinops bannaticus
Erysimum cheiri
Geranium (in variety)
Gunnera manicata
Hemerocallis (in variety)
Inula magnifica
Iris laevigata
Lamium maculatum
Ligularia (in variety)
Nepeta × faassenii
Penstemon (in variety)
Polygonatum × hybridum
Primula florindae
Pulmonaria saccharata
Scabiosa (in variety)
Tradescantia (in variety)
Trollius europaeus
Veronica prostrata
Vinca minor

MOISTURE-LOVING PLANTS

Many gardens have a damp, slightly waterlogged area or perhaps a small pond which can be turned to advantage to grow a wide range of moisture-loving plants. Some, such as bog plants, prefer just a moist soil, others, called aquatics, thrive with their roots actually in water or are grown fully submerged.

ABOVE: Ranunculus acris *'Flore Pleno', the meadow buttercup, growing beside water.*

OPPOSITE: *A shady pond crammed with variegated irises, water and arum lilies and surrounded by ferns, pulmonaria, alchemilla, clematis and hostas. Agapanthus grow in a pot beside the pool.*

ABOVE: *Some irises will grow in water, and some prefer damp soil. They are ideal pool and poolside plants, their tall strappy leaves as important a contribution as their delicate papery flowers. Large-leaved, lush-looking plants like gunnera are spectacular, while, in this planting, ferns and ivy tumble down the brickwork.*

Moisture-loving plants have some special virtues. They are easily grown if you have a permanently damp corner in your garden or a small stream or pond, but for many they provide the incentive to make a pond in the garden or just a boggy area, to convert into a bog garden so that the range of plants in the garden can be extended.

These plants fall into different categories: those that thrive in moist soil, those that thrive in wet soil, and those that actually grow best in water. The plants listed in this section fall into all three categories, but where they actually do well in a depth of water, this is indicated in the entry.

If you already have a damp area of the garden, it is a question of choosing suitable plants for the existing conditions. Quite often, these damp corners are also shady, and any attempt on your part to grow the usual sun-loving perennials will be doomed to disappointment. Analyse the conditions in your garden, and try to learn some lessons from what naturally thrives. Very few bulbs like very wet soil (except those specifically listed here) and will simply rot if water-logged. Plants from dry, rocky areas or from the hot dry areas around the Mediterranean will also fail to cope. Foliage is a good indication of a plant's natural habitat and often plants with larger, greener, lusher leaves have acquired these characteristics from exposure to moist or shady conditions.

A damp garden or corner, therefore, is an opportunity to grow some exciting large foliage plants such as gunneras, rodgersias, rheums and ligularias. If you are making a pond, you can increase your range of plants to those that enjoy being in water, including some of the irises and marsh

Ligularia dentata 'Desdemona'

Giant groundsel
HEIGHT: 4ft (1.2m) • Hardy
FLOWERING SEASON: Mid/late summer

This big herbaceous perennial forms a handsome mound of large, heart-shaped, deep green leaves, with rusty red undersides, borne on the end of long stalks. Big, bright orange, daisy flowers appear in late summer, making a striking contrast with the leaves. In addition to being suited to bog gardens, it makes a good container plant provided the soil is kept moist. It needs humus-rich retentive soil and a sunny or partially shaded site. Divide in spring. Prone to attacks by slugs and snails.

Ligularia stenocephala

Giant groundsel
HEIGHT: 6ft (1.8m) • Hardy
FLOWERING SEASON: Late summer

This cultivar forms similar clumps to *L. dentata* (left), but the leaves are rounded and toothed, and paler green. The yellow-orange daisy-like flowers are borne in long spires on purplish stems. It likes the same conditions as *L. dentata* and looks best when planted in groups of five to seven, in the moist soil around the edge of a water feature. It needs humus-rich retentive soil.

Lobelia cardinalis

Cardinal flower
HEIGHT: 3ft (1m) • Half hardy
FLOWERING SEASON: Summer

This unlikely-looking lobelia bears tall spires of bright red, five-lobed flowers in mid to late summer. The foliage is carried on erect, branching stems. It makes a good border plant in moist soil in partial shade but is not very long-lasting. Grows best in a mild, moist climate with shelter from cold winds and it will grow close to water. Cut down the dead spikes after flowering. Propagate by division in spring. Can be affected by a virus which causes the leaves to mottle and distort.

Lysimachia clethroides

Loosestrife
HEIGHT: 3ft (1m) • Hardy
FLOWERING SEASON: Mid to late summer

This native of China and Japan is a tall summer-flowering perennial with elongated green leaves that turn colour in autumn. It carries small, starry, white flowers with pronounced eyes in long arching spires. It does well in moist soil in sun or partial shade and is most suitable for naturalising by the waterside or in a bog garden. The name comes from the Greek, *lusimachion*, *lysis* meaning concluding or ending, and *mache*, strife, from the reputedly soothing properties of the plant. Divide and replant in autumn.

Lysimachia nummularia

Creeping Jenny/Moneywort
HEIGHT: 2in (5cm) • Hardy
FLOWERING SEASON: Summer

This small creeping perennial, known as moneywort or creeping Jenny, has rounded soft leaves and bright yellow flowers that form in the leaf axils. A cultivar known as 'Aurea' has yellowish-green leaves. It prefers partial shade, and a moist, retentive soil but it is one of the easiest garden plants and can be grown in almost any soil or situation. It is ideal for planting near the borders of a garden pond. Propagate by division in spring or by planting short lengths of the stem in spring or autumn.

Lysimachia punctata

Garden loosestrife
HEIGHT: 3ft (1m) • Hardy
FLOWERING SEASON: Summer

This garden loosestrife is a rapidly spreading, clump-forming, herbaceous perennial. In summer it will produce large drifts of tall, bright golden-yellow flower spires, rising on erect stems above the oval, lance-shaped leaves. *L. punctata* blends well with ligularias in informal bog garden plantings. It prefers moist well-drained soil in partial shade although it will tolerate some sun. It may need staking occasionally. Propagate by division in spring or by seed sown in the open or in a cold frame.

Lysichiton americanus

Yellow skunk cabbage
HEIGHT: 4ft (1.2m) • Hardy
FLOWERING SEASON: Spring

This big-leaved perennial flourishes in the
very moist soil alongside streams and ponds.
It will spread rapidly in the right conditions,
making an eye-catching feature with its
huge, ribbed, mid green leaves and bright
yellow flower spathes about 18in (45cm) tall.
A smaller species, *L. camtschatcensis*, has white
flower spathes. Plant in wet soil or shallow
water, and ensure that the plants have plenty
of humus. Copes with sun or partial shade.
Propagate by division in early spring.

Mertensia pulmonarioides

Virginian cowslip
HEIGHT: 2ft (60cm) • Hardy
FLOWERING SEASON: Late spring

The Virginian cowslip has bluish-grey leaves
and attractive terminal clusters of hanging
purple-blue bells in late spring. It needs a
rich, moist soil in shade to do well. Cut the
plants back in autumn. These plants are
suitable for growing in the shady side of a
rock garden, under deciduous trees or at the
edge of a shrubbery. They do not like being
disturbed but when the clumps grow too
large they can be divided and the roots
replanted in autumn or spring.

Miscanthus sinensis

Zebra grass
HEIGHT: 5ft (1.5m) • Hardy
FLOWERING SEASON: Insignificant

This attractive vigorous giant grass is a hardy
perennial that will serve as a windbreak, its
narrow bluish-green leaves arching over.
There are a number of different cultivars
'Zebrinus' has a yellow band on the leaves,
while 'Gracillimus' has particularly narrow
leaves. It may bear fan-shaped panicles of
hairy white spikelets in the autumn. Plant
in moist garden soil in sun. Cut down to
ground level in late spring. Divide and
replant roots in spring.

Nuphar lutea

Yellow water lily/Brandy bottle
HEIGHT: 2in (5cm) • Hardy
FLOWERING SEASON: Summer

This deep-water aquatic perennial is a good
subject for a large pool. It is vigorous and not
as fussy about sun as the real water lily, and
will grow in running water, which water
lilies will not. The flat, water lily-like leaves
float on the water's surface. In summer it
produces yellow flowers, which are bottle-
shaped, giving rise to the common name
of brandy bottle. Plant in good garden loam
in a sack which is then lowered into the
water. Divide in spring to control its spread.
Propagation is by division in spring.

Nymphaea alba

Water lily
HEIGHT: 2in (5cm) • Hardy
FLOWERING SEASON: Summer

A large water lily, *N. alba*, as the name
implies, has large, pure white flowers which
are semi-double and cup-shaped, with
bright gold stamens. They measure about
4in (10cm) across. Water lilies are deciduous,
perennial, deep water plants and generally
need a 3ft (90cm) depth of water, which
must be still and in sunshine, preferably away
from overhanging trees. It is necessary to
divide the plants every few years in spring or
summer to keep them under control.
Propagation is also by division of rhizomes.

Nymphaea × helvola

Water lily
HEIGHT: 2in (5cm) • Hardy
FLOWERING SEASON: Summer

This small water lily has dark green leaves
which are purple beneath and float on the
surface of the water. It will grow in 12in
(30cm) of water. It bears small, star-shaped,
semi-double yellow flowers in summer. For
best results plant in good loam in a wicker
basket or old-fashioned sack. Like all water
lilies it must be grown in still water and in
sunshine. It is best to remove the foliage of
all water lilies as it dies back. Propagate by
dividing and replanting the rhizomes every
few years.

Nymphaea 'James Brydon'

Water lily
HEIGHT: 2in (5cm) • Hardy
FLOWERING SEASON: Summer

Dark green leaves and fragrant, cup-shaped, rose-coloured, semi-double flowers are the hallmarks of this water lily. White, pink, yellow and purple cultivars are also available, all with characteristically large, semi-double flowers. It needs about a 3ft (1m) depth of water, which must be still and in sunshine. If you want to grow water lilies in a concrete pool you need two barrow loads of soil for each plant. Divide every few years in spring or summer and to propagate.

Nymphoides peltata

Fringed water lily/Water fringe
HEIGHT: 2in (5cm) • Hardy
FLOWERING SEASON: Summer

This deciduous perennial deep-water plant is similar to the water lily, and has the common name fringed water lily. It has dark green, floating, rounded leaves with brown splashed markings and produces small, fringed, yellow flowers throughout the summer. It needs sun and a sheltered site and, like water lilies, likes deep, still water. To propagate, or control its spread, divide in spring or summer.

Osmunda regalis

Royal fern
HEIGHT: 5ft (1.5m) • Hardy
FLOWERING SEASON: Insignificant

This, the royal fern, is an extremely handsome fern, with large, yellowish-green fronds arching over gracefully, growing out of a crown that gradually becomes like a small trunk. There are a couple of interesting varieties, *O. r.* Cristata Group has crested pinnae, and *O. r. purpurascens* has young fronds which are bronzy-pink. The royal fern does well in very damp soil near pond margins. Propagate by dividing well-separated crowns in spring.

Polystichum setiferum

Soft shield fern
HEIGHT: 3ft (1m) • Hardy
FLOWERING SEASON: Insignificant

The soft shield fern, a native of temperate and tropical regions throughout the world, has large soft-textured fronds which are finely divided and mid green in colour. It will naturalize in damp conditions. There are several named cultivars, including 'Divisilobum Laxum' which has huge fronds with white scales when young, these arch initially and become prostrate later. It is best to grow these ferns in shade in humus-rich, moisture-retentive soil. Propagate by dividing the crowns in spring.

Pontederia cordata

Pickerel weed
HEIGHT: 2ft (60cm) • Hardy
FLOWERING SEASON: Late summer

The pickerel weed, as it is commonly known, is a vigorous, aquatic perennial that will grow in up to 9in (23cm) of water. It has glossy green, heart-shaped leaves, rather like those of an arum lily, and produces small, bright blue flowers with a yellow eye in late summer. It needs full sun, and should be planted in loam. It is a good idea to remove the flower heads as they fade to encourage further flowering. Divide the plant in late spring and replant in shallow water until the plants are established.

Populus × *canadensis* 'Serotina'

Canadian poplar
HEIGHT: 36ft (11m) • Hardy
FLOWERING SEASON: Spring

This is a quick-growing tree with oval, pointed leaves that are coppery red when juvenile, turning dark green later. There is a golden-leaved cultivar, 'Aurea', which turns a very bright yellow in autumn. It bears long red catkins in the spring and should be planted well away from buildings as the branches are somewhat brittle and often break off in very strong winds. Propagate from hardwood cuttings in autumn. May be attacked by aphids and suffer various fungal disorders.

Primula florindae

Giant cowslip/Himalayan cowslip
HEIGHT: 6ft (1.8m) • Hardy
FLOWERING SEASON: Spring

This giant cowslip, also known as the Himalayan cowslip, originates in Tibet and China. It has large, heart-shaped leaves with serrated edges on a fairly long leaf stalk. In spring, tall stems bear umbels of scented, bell-shaped, pale lemon flowers on drooping stalks. Forms are also available with orange or red flowers. These primulas prefer sun or partial shade and moist soil but may require protection from winter wet. Divide to propagate. Prone to rots and moulds.

Primula pulverulenta

Candelabra primula
HEIGHT: 3ft (1m) • Hardy
FLOWERING SEASON: Summer

These tall, candelabra-type primulas look attractive in large drifts near a pond or a stream. They have the typical oval, primrose-type leaves in pale green while the flowers are deep reddish-purple carried in a whorl at the top of long white stems. *P. p.* Bartley Hybrids and *P. p.* 'Bartley Pink' are soft pink in colour with a deeper crimson eye. *P. pulverulenta* does best in sun or partial shade and prefers rich loamy soil. Propagate named forms by dividing crowns or by removing offsets in spring. They are prone to attacks by aphids and various moulds.

Ranunculus acris 'Flore Pleno'

Double meadow buttercup
HEIGHT: 18in (45cm) • Hardy
FLOWERING SEASON: Summer

This is double-flowered buttercup is sometimes also known as yellow bachelor's buttons. It produces large, bright yellow, saucer-shaped flowers in sprays and has deeply cut, lobed, mid green leaves. This widely grown species is mat-forming but not invasive. It thrives in moist, well-drained soil and prefers to be in sun or partial shade. Once established, it needs little attention. To propagate, divide and replant the clumps in autumn or in spring.

Ranunculus aquatilis

Water crowfoot
HEIGHT: 2ft (60cm) • Hardy
FLOWERING SEASON: Spring/midsummer

This water crowfoot is an aquatic plant which can be grown in water up to 12in (30cm) deep and will grow in slow-moving streams. It has myriads of white blossoms in the spring which cover the surface of the water, looking like miniature water lilies. It has two types of leaf, floating leaves carried on long stems which are smooth and round and submerged leaves which are finely divided and hair-like. Plant in the sun. *R. aquatilis* is very vigorous and will need to be divided and thinned annually.

Rheum palmatum

Ornamental rhubarb
HEIGHT: 6ft (1.8m) • Hardy
FLOWERING SEASON: Summer

This ornamental rhubarb is an excellent large perennial for a bog garden and forms a huge and spectacular plant. It produces a pyramid-shaped clump of large, deeply cut, rhubarb-like leaves that open reddish purple and turn green. The flowers, which are rusty pink, are carried at the end of tall spires in midsummer. Plant in humus-rich soil in partial shade and mulch each autumn. Do not let the soil dry out in the growing season. Generally pest and disease-free, but can be prone to aphid attacks.

Sagittaria sagittifolia

Common arrowhead
HEIGHT: 3ft (1m) • Hardy
FLOWERING SEASON: Summer

The common arrowhead can be planted in water of depths up to 3ft (90cm). A hardy perennial, it has arrow-shaped, light green leaves and whorls of white flowers in summer. *S. s.* 'Flore Pleno' is a double-flowered variety. Plant in early spring or mid-autumn in any good garden soil enriched with well-rotted manure. Put the soil in an old-fashioned sack or wicker basket, plant the tubers, weigh the soil down with a large stone and then drop it into the pool. It likes full sun. Thin in the summer.

Stratiotes aloides

Water soldier/Crab's claw
HEIGHT: 6in (15cm) ◆ Hardy
FLOWERING SEASON: Summer

This semi-evergreen perennial, known as
the water soldier, is a submerged aquatic,
which floats freely in any depth of water. It
has strappy, fleshy, olive-green leaves in a
rosette formation, and produces small, cup-
shaped, white flowers in summer. During
winter the plants lie dormant on the pool
bottom. The plant spreads quickly and may
well need to be controlled in a garden pool.
Propagation is by division of the plants in
spring.

Trapa natans

Jesuit's nut/Water chestnut
HEIGHT: 1in (2.5cm) ◆ Half-hardy
FLOWERING SEASON: Summer

This annual aquatic plant,which is sometimes known as the Jesuit's nut or water
chestnut, has pretty triangular leaves, with
serrated edges,that are marked with bronze-
purple splashes. It produces white flowers in
summer. It is not reliably frost-hardy so the
young plants will require some degree of
protection if planted in early spring, or
plant when the last frosts have passed.
Propagation is by division of the plants in
spring or by seed.

Typha latifolia

Reed mace/Bulrush
HEIGHT: 6ft (1.8m) ◆ Hardy
FLOWERING SEASON: Summer

This marginal reed is grown for its long,
strappy, mid green leaves and its decorative
dark brown cylinders of seed heads in
autumn. The beige flowers which emerge in
midsummer are not particularly significant
but the seed heads are spectacular and a common sight, often used by flower arrangers. It
is invasive, and is often used to colonize large
ponds and lakes. To control its spread plant it
in a tub. It will do well in sun or shade, and
can be propagated by division in spring.

More Plants for Moisture

AQUATICS
Examples of the majority of aquatic plants,
plants that like growing with their roots in
water, have been included in this chapter.
There is a wide choice of water lilies and if
you plan to make a pond, it is best to visit a
nursery which specializes in plants for the
water garden. It is worth stressing that water
lilies must be grown in deep, still water and
a sunny position.

Other suitable aquatic plants worth
considering include:

Alisma plantago-aquatica (Water plantain)
Azolla filiculoides (Water fern)
Lagarosiphon major
Myosotis scorpioides (Water forget-me-not)
Myriophyllum aquaticum (Parrot's feather)
  M. verticillatum (Water milfoil)
Orontium aquaticum (Golden club)
Potamogeton crispus (Curled pondweed)

PLANTS FOR MOISTURE

If you have a very wet area of your garden
then you have to grown plants that will
tolerate these conditions. All plants need
water but a relatively small number will
survive in conditions of constant moisture.

Bog garden plants are obvious examples.
Plants that will survive in swampy sites are
marked (S).

TREES

Abies (in variety)
Acer negundo
Alnus (in variety)
Amelanchier canadensis
Betula nigra
Crataegus (in variety)
Embothrium coccineum
Fraxinus angustifolia
Liquidambar styraciflua
Liriodendron tulipifera
Parrotia persica
Populus (in variety) (S)
Prunus padus
Pterocarya fraxinifolia (S)
Salix (in variety) (S)
Sambucus (in variety) (S)
Taxodium distichum (S)
Tsuga heterophylla

SHRUBS

Aucuba japonica
Camellia (in variety)
Clethra arborea
Cornus (in variety)
Desfontainia spinosa,
Elaeagnus × ebbingei
Fatsia japonica

Hydrangea (in variety)
Osmanthus (in variety)
Sarcococca hookeriana
Skimmia japonica
Symphoricarpus × doorenbosii
Viburnum davidii
Zenobia pulverulenta

PERENNIALS & GROUND COVER PLANTS

Ajuga reptans
Alchemilla mollis
Anemone × hybrida cvs
Aruncus dioicus
Astilbe (in variety)
Bergenia (in variety)
Campanula persicifolia
Cardamine pratensis
Convallaria majalis
Darmera peltata (S)
Dodecatheon pulchellum
Enkianthus campanulatus
Filipendula palmata
Helleborus orientalis
Hosta (in variety)
Houttuynia cordata (S)
Iris pseudacorus (S)
Kirengeshoma palmata
Mentha (in variety)
Menziesia ciliicalyx
Persicaria bistorta
Polypodium vulgare (S)
Rheum palmatum
Rodgersia pinnata (S)
Trillium grandiflorum

Index of Plants

Italic numerals show plants that are illustrated. ® Registered Name or Selling Name.

Abelia × *grandiflora* 23, 72
Abies 91
   A. koreana 40, 67
Acantholimon glumaceum 14
Acanthus spinosus 9, 23, 56
Acer 35, 51, 67, 79
   A. campestre 35
   A. negundo 91
      A. n. 'Flamingo' *56*
      A. n. var. *violaceum* 56
      A. n. 'Varigatum' 56
   A. palmatum 9
      A. p. var. *dissectum* 'Ornatum' *26*
   A. platanoides 35, 72
      A. p. 'Crimson King' 72
      A. p. 'Drummondii' 72
   A. rubrum 40
Achillea filipendulina 23
   A. f. 'Gold Plate' *56*
Aconitum
   A. 'Blue Sceptre' 28
   A. 'Bressingham Spire' *28*, 51
Acorus
   A. calamus 'Variegatus' *84*
   A. gramineus 'Variegatus' *84*
Actinidia kolomikta 9, *56*
Adam's needle *see Yucca filamentosa*
Adiantum pedatum 28
   A. p. 'Asiatic' 28
   A. p. var. *subpumilum* 28

Aesculus
   A. hippocastamum 56
   A. pavia 56
      A. p. 'Atrosanguinea' 56
      A. p. 'Humilis' 56
Aethionema 'Warley Ruber' *14*
African lily *see Agapanthus*
Agapanthus 9
   A. Headbourne Hybrids *14*
Ajuga reptans 28, 91
   A. r. 'Atropurpurea' 28
   A. r. 'Braunherz' 28
   A. r. 'Burgundy Glow' 28
Alcea rosea Chater's Double Group 72
Alchemilla 27
   A. alpina 28
   A. mollis 25, 28, 51, 67, 79, 91
Alisma plantago-aquatica 91
Alnus 35, 91
   A. incana 35, 51, 72
      A. i. 'Aurea' 72
alpine columbine *see Aquilegia alpina*
alpine heath *see Erica carnea*
Amaranthus
   A. caudatus 72
      A. c. 'Viridis' 72
   A. tricolor var. *salicifolius* 72
Amelanchier 9
   A. canadensis 51, *56*, 79, 91
Amenome × *hybrida* 67
American cowslip *see Dodecatheon pulchellum*
Anchusa
   A. azurea 23, 57

A. a. 'Loddon Royalist' 57
A. a. 'Opal' 57
Andromeda polifolia 'Compacta' *40*
Anemone
   A. hupehensis var. *japonica*
      'Bressingham Glow' 72
   A. × *hybrida* 79, 91
      A. × *h.* 'Honorine Jobert' 72
      A. × *h.* 'Königin Charlotte' 72
Anthemis
   A. punctata ssp. *cupaniana 13, 14*
   A. tinctoria 27
Aponogeton distachyos 84
Aquilegia
   A. alpina 51, *57*, 79
   A. vulgaris 57
Aralia
   A. elata 73
      A. e. 'Aureovariegata' 73
Arbutus 9
   A. × *andrachnoides* 40, 79
Arctostaphylos uva-ursi 40
Aristolochia durior 40
Arizona cypress *see Cupressus arizonica* var. *glabra* 'Blue Ice'
Aronia arbutifolia 51, 67, 73
Artemesia absinthium 23, 51, 67, 79
Aruncus dioicus 51, 67, 73, 91
ash-leaved maple *see Acer negundo*
Asplenium scolopendrium 84
   Crispum Group 84
   Cristatum Group 84
Aster novi-belgii 67, 79
   A. n.-b. 'Jenny' *14*
   A. n.-b. 'Royal Ruby' 14
   A. n.-b. 'White Ladies' 14
Astilbe 35, 67, 91
   A. 'Bressingham Beauty' 73
   A. 'Feuer' 73
   A. × *arendsii* 73
Astilboides tabularis 84
Astrantia major 51, *57*, 79
Aucuba 9
   A. japonica 26, 35, 51, *57*, 79, 91
      A. j. 'Crotonifolia' 57
      A. j. 'Picturata' 57
Australian tree fern *see Dicksonia antarctica*
Azolla filiculoides 91
azure sage *see Perovskia atriplicifolia*

baby's breath *see Gypsophila* 'Rosenschleier'
bald cypress *see Taxodium distichum*
balm of Gilead *see Populus* × *candicans*
bamboo *see Phyllostachys viridiglaucescens*
barberry *see Berberis* × *stenophylla*
barrenwort *see Epimedium grandiflorum*
Bashania 35
bearberry *see Arctostaphylos uva-ursi*
beard tongue *see Penstemon* 'Apple Blossom'
bear's breeches *see Acanthus spinosus*
beauty bush *see Kolkwitzia amabilis*
Begonia
   B. rex
      B. r. 'Merry Christmas' 28
      B. r. 'Princess of Hanover' 28
      Hybrids 28, 35
   B. x carrierei 41
bellflower *see Campanula lactiflora*
bellwort *see Uvularia grandiflora*
Berberidopsis corallina 41
Berberis 9, 23, 35, 51, 67, 79
   B. darwinii 57
   B. × *stenophylla* 73
      B. × *s.* 'Crawley Gem' 73
Bergenia 9, 35, 67, 79, 91
   B. cordifolia 51
Betula 35, 91
   B. ermanii 79
   B. nigra 35, 91
   B. pendulata 35
bilberry *see Vaccinium corymbosum*
birthwort *see Aristolochia durior*
bitter cress *see Cardamine pratensis*
black false hellebore *see Veratrum nigrum*
black mulberry *see Morus nigra*

bladder nut *see Staphylea colchica*
bleeding heart *see Dicentra spectabilis* 'Alba'
blue alkanet *see Anchusa azurea*
blue cupidone *see Catananche caerulea*
blue poppy *see Meconopsis betonicifolia*
blueberry *see Vaccinium corymbosum*
bog arum *see Calla palustris*
bog iris *see Iris ensata*
Bowles golden sedge *see Carex elata*
box elder *see Acer negundo* 'Flamingo'
Boxus sempervirens 9
Brachyglottis Dunedin Hybrids Group 'Sunshine' *see Senecio* 'Sunshine'
brandy bottle *see Nuphar lutea*
bride bush *see Exochorda* × *macrantha* 'The Bride'
broom *see Cytisus* × *kewensis; Genista aetnensis*
Brunnera
   B. macrophylla 28, 57
   B. m. 'Dawson's White' 57
   B. m. 'Hadspen Cream' 28
Buddleja 51, 67, 79
   B. alternifolia 14
      B. a. 'Argentea' 14
   B. davidii 7
bugle *see Ajuga reptans*
bulrush *see Typha latifolia*
burning bush *see Dictamnus albus* var. *purpureus*
bush honeysuckle *see Weigela florida* 'Foliis Purpureis'
busy lizzies *see Impatiens*
Butomus umbellatus 84
butterfly bush *see Buddleja alternifolia*
Buxus sempervirens 23, 35

calico bush *see Kalmia latifolia*
Californian fuchsia *see Zauschneria californica*
Californian lilac *see Ceanothus impressus*
Californian tree poppy *see Romneya coulteri*
Calla palustris 85
callery pear *see Pyrus calleryana*
Calluna 9
   C. vulgaris
      C. v. 'J H Hamilton' *41*
      C. v. 'Sunrise' 41
Caltha palustris 85
   C. p. var. *alba* 85
Camellia 9, 35, 91
   C. japonica 'R L Wheller' *41*
   C. × *williamsii* 'Donation' *41*
camomile *see Anthemis punctata* ssp. *cupaniana*
Campanula 51
   C. carpatica 67, 79
   C. lactiflora 35, 58
      C. l. 'Loddon Anna' 58
      C. l. 'Prichard's Variety' 58
   C. persicifolia 15, 91
      C. p. var. *planiflora* f. *alba* 15
Campsis 9
   C. × *tagliabuana* 'Mme Galen' *58*
Campsis radicans 23, 73
Canadian poplar *see Populus* × *canadensis* 'Serotina'
Canary Island ivy *see Hedera canariensis* 'Gloire de Marengo'
Candelabra primular *see Primula pulverulenta*
Cape figwort *see Phygelius capensis*
cape pondweed *see Aponogeton distachyos*
Cardamine pratensis 91
   C. p. 'Flore Pleno' 74
cardinal flower *see Lobelia cardinalis*
Carex
   C. buchananii 29
   C. elata 23
      C. e. 'Aurea' *29*
   C. pendula 29
carnation *see Dianthus* 'Doris'
Carpentaria californica 23
Carpinus betulus 23, 51, 67
Caryopteris × *clandonensis* 23

   C. × *c.* 'Heavenly Blue' *58*
Cassiope 'Muirhead' *41*
Catalpa bignonioides 15, 67, 79
   C. b. 'Aurea' 15
Catananche
   C. caerulea 15, 67
      C. c. 'Major' 15
      C. c. 'Perry's White' 15
   C. centaurea 23
catmint *see Nepeta* × *faassenii*
Caucasian wing nut *see Pterocarya fraxinifolia*
Ceanothus 23, 51
   C. impressus 58
Celastrus orbiculatus 74
Centaurea cyanus 23
Centhranthus, C. ruber 23, 51, *58*, 79
Ceratostigma willmottianum 23, 51, 67
Cercidiphyllum 9

C. japonicum 42, 67, 79
Cercis 9
   C. siliquastrum 58
Chaenomeles 79
   C. japonica 67, 74
chalk plant *see Gypsophila repens* 'Rosa Schönheit'; *Gypsophila* 'Rosenschleier'
Chamaecyparis lawsoniana 51
Chilean fire bush *see Embothrium coccineum*
Chilean glory flower *see Eccremocarpus scaber*
Chimonanthus praecox 67, 79
Choisya ternata 29, 51, 67, 79
chokeberry *see Aronia arbutifolia*
Christmas rose *see Helleborus orientalis*
cider gum *see Eucalyptus gunnii*
Cistus 12
   C. albidus 59
   C. creticus 59
   C. × *cyprius* 23, *59*
Clarkia
   C. elegans 15
      C. e. 'Love Affair' 15
Clematis 35
   C. tangutica 23
   C. texensis 59
   C. 'The Princess of Wales' 59
Clethra arborea 35, *42*, 91
climbing hydrangea *see Hydrangea anomala* subsp. *petiolaris*
cobnut *see Corylus avellana* 'Contorta'
Colorado spruce *see Picea pungens*
columbine *see Aquilegia alpina*
comfrey *see Symphytum* × *uplandicum*
common arrowhead *see Sagittaria sagittifolia*
common German flag *see Iris germanica*
Convallaria majalis 91
Convolvulus cneorum 11, 15
coral plant *see Berberidopsis corallina*
cornflower *see Centaurea cyanus*
Cornus 35, 51, 67, 79, 91
   C. alba 'Sibirica' *85*
   C. canadensis 42
   C. kousa
      C. k. 'Satomi' 42
      C. k. var. *chinensis* 42
   C. nuttallii 42

C. n. 'Gold Spot' 42
Coronilla valentina ssp. *glauca* 23
Cortaderia selloana
    C. s. 'Aureolineata' 15
    C. s. 'Sunningdale Silver' 15
Corydalis
    C. cheilanthifolia 42
    C. lutea 59
Corylopsis pauciflora 43
Corylus 67
    C. avellana 'Contorta' 16, 79
Cotinus coggygria 51, 67, 79
Cotoneaster horizontalis 23, 35
cowberry *see Vaccinium corymbosum*
crab's claw *see Stratiotes aloides*
Crambe
    C. cordifolia 23, 67, 74
    C. maritima 74
cranesbill *see Geranium* 'Johnson's Blue'
Crataegus 9, 35, 51, 67, 79, 91
    C. crus-galli 29
    C. laciniata 16
    C. laevigata
        C. l. 'Paul's Scarlet' 59
        C. l. 'Punicea' 29
    C. persimilis 'Prunifolia' 29
    C. × lavalleei 29
creeping dogwood *see Cornus canadensis*
creeping Jenny *see Lysimachia nummularia*
Crocosmia 'Lucifer' 23
Cryptomeria japonica 43
    C. j. 'Elegans' 43
cuckoo flower *see Cardamine pratensis*
    'Flore Pleno'; *Lychnis flos-cuculi*
cupid's dart *see Catananche caerulea*
Cupressus arizonica
    C. a. var. *glabra* 'Blue Ice' 59
    C. a. var. *glabra* 'Compacta' 59
curled pondweed *see Potamogeton crispus*
curry plant *see Helichrysum italicum*
Cyperus involucratus 85
    C. i. 'Variegatus' 85
Cypripedium reginae 43
Cytisus 54
    C. battandieri 16
    C. × kewensis 16

Daboecia cantabrica 43
    D. c. 'Snowdrift' 43
daisy bush *see Senecio* 'Sunshine'
Darlingtonia californica 43
Darmera peltata 74, 91
Darwin's barberry *see Berberis darwinii*
Davidia involucrata 16, 67
day lily *see Hemerocallis dumortieri*
Delphinium 'Lord Butler' 59
Desfontainia spinosa 35, 43, 91
    D. s. 'Harold Comber' 43
Deutzia scabra
    D. s. 'Candidissima' 60
    D. s. 'Plena' 60
devil-in-a-bush *see Nigella damascena*
Dianthus 23, 67, 79
    D. 'Doris' 60
Diascia fetcaniensis 16
Dicentra 35, 67, 79
    D. formosa 29
    D. spectabilis 'Alba' 29
Dicksonia antarctica 29
Dictamnus albus var. *purpureus* 12
Digitalis 61, 79
    D. grandiflora 74
    D. purpurea 29
Dodecatheon pulchellum 35, 75, 91
dog fennel *see Anthemis punctata* ssp.
    cupaniana
dogwood *see Cornus kousa* var. *chinensis*
Doronicum
    D. plantagineum 60
    D. × excelsum
    D. × e. 'Harpur Crewe' 60
    D. × e. 'Miss Mason' 60
    D. × e. 'Spring Beauty' 60
Dorotheanthus bellidiformis 17
double meadow buttercup *see Ranunculus*
    acris 'Flore Pleno'
Douglas fir *see Pseudotsuga menziesii*

dove tree *see Davidia involucrata*
dragon's claw willow *see Salix babylonica*
    var. *pekinensis*
dropwort *see Filipendula palmata* 'Alba'
Dryas octopetala 60
Dryopteris filix-mas 30
Dutchman's pipe *see Aristolochia durior*
Dutchman's trousers *see Dicentra spectabilis*
    'Alba'

eastern white cedar *see Thuja occidentalis*
    'Sunkist'
Eccremocarpus 9
    E. scaber 23, 60
    E. scaber aurantiacus 60
    E. scaber roseus 60
Echinops
    E. bannaticus 51, 67, 79
    E. b. 'Taplow Blue' 17
Elaeagnus × *ebbingei* 91
    E. × e. 'Gilt Edge' 30
Embothrium coccineum 35, 44, 91
    Lanceolatum Group 44
Enkianthus campanulatus 44, 91
Enonymus fortunei 67
Epimedium 9
    E. grandiflorum 30, 35, 44
    E. g. 'Rose Queen' 30
Eremurus
    E. himalaicus 60
    E. robusta 60
    E. × isabellinus Shelford Hybrids 60

Erica 38
    E. carnea
        E. c. 'Aurea' 44
        E. c. 'Springwood White' 44
    E. cinerea 'Golden Drop' 44
    E. × darleyensis
        E. × d. 'Darley Dale' 44
        E. × d. 'Kramer's Red' 44
        E. × d. 'Silberschmelze' 44
Eryngium
    E. bourgatii 17
    E. giganteum 12
Erysimum cheiri 61, 79
Escallonia 9, 67
    E. 'Slieve Donard' 17
Etna broom *see Genista aetnensis*
Eucalyptus gunnii 17
Eucryphia
    E. lucida 'Pink Cloud' 44
    E. × nymansensis 'Nymansay' 44
Euonymus fortunei 23, 35, 51, 67
Euphorbia 23
    E. amygdaloides var. *robbiae* 30
evening primrose *see Oenothera*
    missouriensis
everlasting pea *see Lathyrus*
    grandiflorus
Exochorda × *macrantha* 'The Bride' 61,
    79

Fagus 51, 67
    F. sylvatica 54
false Solomon's seal *see Smilacina racemosa*
false spikenard *see Smilacina racemosa*
Fatsia japonica 26, 30, 91
Festuca 9
Ficus carica 9, 67, 79

fig marigold *see Dorotheanthus bellidiformis*
Filipendula 9
    F. palmata 51, 85, 91
        F. p. 'Alba' 74
    F. vulgaris 'Multiplex' 75
firethorn *see Pyracantha* 'Orange Glow'
flame creeper *see Tropaeolum speciosum*
fleabane *see Inula magnifica*
flower-of-a-day *see Tradescantia* ×
    andersoniana 'Purple Dome'
flowering rush *see Butomus umbellatus*
Forsythia suspensa 35, 51, 61, 79
Fothergilla major 91
foxglove *see Digitalis*
foxtail lily *see Eremurus himalaicus*
Fraxinus angustifolia 67, 79, 91
Fremontodendron 'California Glory' 23
fringe cup *see Tellima grandiflora*
fringed water lily *see Nymphoides peltata*
frogbit *see Hydrocharis morsus-ranae*
Fuchsia 'Golden Dawn' 30
fumitory *see Corydalis cheilanthifolia;*
    Corydalis lutea

Galium odoratum 35, 51
Galtonia candicans 17
garden loosestrife *see Lysimachia punctata*
Garryea 9
    G. elliptica 35
Gaultheria 9, 35
    G. mucronata 45
        G. m. 'Bell's Seedling' 45
        G. m. 'Lilacina' 45
    G. shallon 45
Genista 24, 54
    G. aetnensis 12, 18
gentian *see Gentiana sino-ornata*
Gentiana
    G. asclepiadea 31
    G. sino-ornata 45
Geranium 23, 51, 67, 79
    G. clarkei 7
    G. endressii 61
    G. 'Johnson's Blue' 61
    G. palmatum 31
    G. phaeum 31, 71
    G. pratense 61
        G. p. 'Mrs Kendall Clark' 61
giant cowslip *see Primula florindae*
giant groundsel *see Ligularia dentata;*
    Ligularia stenocephala
Ginkgo biloba 75
Gleditsia 9, 54
    G. triacanthos 35
        G. t. 'Rubylace' 18
        G. t. 'Sunburst' 18
globe flower *see Trollius europaeus*
globe thistle *see Echinops bannaticus*
goat willow *see Salix caprea*
goat's beard *see Aruncus dioicus; Astilbe* ×
    arendsii
golden bell *see Forsythia suspensa*
golden club *see Orontium aquaticum*
golden hop *see Humulus lupulus* 'Aureus'
golden larch *see Pseudolarix amabilis*
golden oats *see Stipa gigantea*
golden-rain tree *see Koelreuteria paniculata*
granny's bonnets *see Aquilegia vulgaris*
grey alder *see Alnus incana*
gromwell *see Lithodora diffusa*
Guelder rose *see Viburnum opulus*
gum cistus *see Cistus* × *cyprius*
Gunnera manicata 51, 79, 85
Gypsophila 23
    G. paniculata 'Bristol Fairy' 61
    G. repens
        G. r. 'Rosa Schönheit' 18
        G. r. 'Rosea' 18, 61
    G. 'Rosenschleier' 61

Halesia monticola 45
× *Halimiocistus wintonensis* 18
Hamamelis 9
    H. mollis 51
    H. × intermedia 45
        H. x i. 'Diane' 45
        H. x i. 'Ruby Glow' 45

handkerchief tree *see Davidia involucrata*
hart's tongue fern *see Asplenium*
    scolopendrium
hawthorn *see Crataegus*
hazelnut *see Corylus avellana*
heather *see Erica*
Hebe pinguifolia 'Pagei' 23
Hedera
    H. algeriensis 'Ravensholst' 31
    H. canariensis 'Gloire de
        Marengo' 31
Helianthemum 67
    H. 'Amy Baring' 18
    H. 'Rhodanthe Carneum' 18
    H. 'Wisley Primrose' 18
    H. 'Wisley White' 18
Helichrysum italicum 18
Helleborus orientalis 31, 91
Hemerocallis 79
    H. 'Burning Daylight' 75
    H. dumortieri 86
    H. fulva
        H. f. 'Flore Pleno' 75
        H. f. 'Kwanso Variegata' 75
    H. lilioasphodelus 86
hepatica anemone *see Hepatica nobilis*
Hepatica nobilis 31
Hibiscus syriacus
    H. s. 'Oiseau Bleu' 19
    H. s. 'Red Heart' 19
    H. s. 'Woodbridge' 19
Himalayan cowslip *see Primula florindae*
Hippophae rhamnoides 23, 35
Holboellia coriacea 46
holly *see Ilex aquifolium*
hollyhock *see Alcea rosea*
honey locust *see Gleditsia triacanthos*
    'Sunburst'
hop hornbeam *see Ostrya carpinifolia*
horse chesnut *see Aesculus pavia*
Hosta 9, 91
    H. crispula 70
    H. fortunei 31
        H. f. var. *albopicta* 31
        H. f. var. *aureomarginata* 31
    H. sieboldiana var. *elegans* 32, 75
    H. 'Spinners' 75
Hottonia palustris 86
Houttuynia cordata 35, 91
    H. c. 'Chameleon' 69, 75
    H. c. 'Flore Pleno' 75
Humulus lupulus 'Aureus' 76
Hydrangea 91
    H. anomala subsp. *petiolaris* 32
    H. aspera Villosa Group 62
    H. macrophylla 'Générale Vicomtesse
        de Vibray' 46
    H. petiolaris 35
hydrangea vine *see Schizophragma*
    integrifolium
Hydrocharis morsus-ranae 86
Hypericum
    H. 'Hidcote' 19
    H. 'Hidcote Variegated' 19
    H. × inodorum 'Elstead' 32

ice plant *see Dorotheanthus bellidiformis*
Ilex 9
    I. aquifolium 35
        I. a. 'Silver Queen' 19
    I. × altaclernsis 'Gold King' 19

Impatiens New Guinea Hybrids *32*
Imperata 9
Indian bean tree *see Catalpa bignonioides*
indigo *see Indigofera heterantha*
Indigofera heterantha 23, *46*
Inula magnifica 79, 86, *86*
Ipomea hederacea 23
Iris 67
    I. 'Black Swan' 62
    I. ensata 86
      I. e. 'Alba' 86
      I. e. 'Variegata' 86
    I. foetidissima 35
    I. germanica 23, 51, *62*
    I. laevigata 79, *86*
      I. l. 'Alba' 86
      I. l. 'Atropurpurea' 86
      I. l. 'Regal' 86
      I. l. 'Variegata' 86
    I. pseudacorus 9, 35, 76, 91
      I. p. 'Variegata' 76
    I. 'Wabash' 62

Japanese anemone *see Anemone × hybrida*
Japanese angelica tree *see Aralia elata*
Japanese cedar *see Cryptomeria japonica*
Japanese flag *see Iris ensata*
Japanese iris *see Iris laevigata*
Japanese quince *see Chaenomeles japonica*

japonica *see Chaenomeles japonica*
Jasmium
    J. nudiflorum 35
    J. officinale 51, 67
Jerusalem cross *see Lychnis chalcedonica*
Jerusalem sage *see Phlomis fruticosa*
Jesuit's nut *see Tarpa natans*
Jew's mallow *see Kerria japonica*
Joseph's coat *see Amaranthus caudatus*
Judas tree *see Cercis siliquastrum*
Juniperus
    J. communis 23
    J. scopulorum 'Skyrocket' *62*
    J. virgiana 'Sulphur Spray' *62*

Kalmia latifolia 9, 35, *37, 46*
    K. l. 'Silver Dollar' *46*
    K. l. var. *alba 46*
Katsura tree *see Cercidiphyllum japonicum*
Kerria japonica 35
    K. j. 'Pleniflora' *62*
king's spear *see Eremurus himalaicus*
Kirengeshoma palmata 46, 91
Kniphofia
    K. 'Little Maid' *19*
    K. 'Royal Standard' *19*
    K. 'Samuel's Sensation' *19*
    K. 'Sunningdale Yellow' 23
knotweed *see Persicaria bistorta*
Koelreuteria paniculata 46, 67
Kolkwitzia amabilis 62
Korean fir *see Abies koreana*

Laburnum 9
    L. × watereri 'Vossii' *19*
lady's mantle *see Alchemilla mollis*
lady's smock *see Cardamine pratensis*
Lagarosiphon major 91
lamb's tongue *see Stachys byzantina*
Lamium maculatum 23, 35, 51, 67, 79

Lapageria rosea 51
Larix decidua 51, 67
Lathyrus 9, 54
    L. grandiflorus 76
    L. latifolius 'White Pearl' 76
laurustinus *see Viburnum tinus*
Lavandula 9, 67, 79
    L. angustifolia 20
      L. a. 'Alba' 20
      L. a. 'Hidcote' 20
      L. a. 'Rosea' 20
    L. stoechas 8
Lavatera
    L. 'Barnsley' 51, *62*, 79
    L. 'Rosea' 62
lavender *see Lavandula angustifolia*
Lenten rose *see Helleborus orientalis*
leopard's bane *see Doronicum plantagineum*
Leucanthemum × superbum 67, 76
    L. × s. 'Snowcap' 76
    L. × s. 'Wirral Supreme' 76
Leucothoe fontanesiana 35, 47
    L. f. 'Rainbow' 47
Ligularia 51, 79
    L. dentata 'Desdemona' *87*
    L. stenocephala 87
Ligustrum ovalifolium 51, 67, 79
lilac *see Syringa × henryi*
Lilium 9
lily tree *see Magnolia × soulangeana*
lily-of-the-valley tree of Madeira *see Clethra arborea*
lilyturf *see Liriope muscari*
ling *see Calluna vulgaris*
Linum narbonense 54
Liquidambar styraciflua 79, 91
    L. s. 'Worplesdon' *47*, 67
Liriodendron tulipifera 51, 91
Liriope muscari 20
    L. m. 'Curly Twist' *20*
    L. m. 'Variegata' *20*
Lithodora diffusa 'Heavenly Blue' *20*
Livingstone daisy *see Dorotheanthus bellidiformis*
Lobelia cardinalis 87
Lonicera
    L. japonica 'Halliana' 23
    L. periclymenum 63
    L. pileata 35
    L. × brownii 'Dropmore Scarlet' *63*
loosestrife *see Lysimachia clethroides*
love-in-a-mist *see Nigella damascena*
love-lies-bleeding *see Amaranthus caudatus*
Lupinus
    L. luteus 47
    Russell Hybrids *63*
Lychnis
    L. chalcedonica 20
      L. c. 'Alba' *20*
    L. coronaria 8
    L. flos-cuculi 20
Lysichiton
    L. americanus 88
    L. camtschatcensis 88
Lysimachia
    L. clethroides 87
    L. nummularia 87
      L. n. 'Aurea' *87*
    L. punctata 23, *87*

Macleaya microcarpa 20
Magnolia
    M. acuminata 47
    M. campbellii 47
    M. delavayi 47
    M. denudata 47
    M. grandiflora 47, 51
    M. kobus 47
    M. stellata 47
    M. wilsonii 47
    M. × soulangeana 'Lennei' *47*
Mahonia 9, 51, 67, 79
    M. aquifolium 'Atropurpurea' *32*
maidenhair fern *see Thalictrum aquilegiifolium* var. *album*
maidenhair tree *see Ginkgo biloba*
male fern *see Dryopteris filix-mas*

Maltese cross *see Lychnis chalcedonica*
Malus 67, 79
marsh marigold *see Caltha palustris*
masterwort *see Astrantia major*
Matteuccia struthiopteris 27, *32*
may *see Crataegus laevigata* 'Punicea'
meadow cranesbill *see Geranium pratense*
meadow rue *see Thalictrum aquilegiifolium* var. *album*
meadowsweet *see Filipendula palmata; Spiraea betulifolia*
Meconopsis
    M. betonicifolia 47
    M. cambrica 27, *33*
Mentha 91
    M. suavolens 35
Menziesia ciliicalyx 91
    M. c. 'Spring Morning' 48
    M. c. var. *purpurea* 48
merry-bells *see Uvularia grandiflora*
Mertensia pulmonarioides 88
Mexican orange blossom *see Choisya ternata*
Michaelmas daisy *see Aster novi-belgii*
milkwort *see Euphorbia amygdaloides*
Mimulus × burnetii 76
Miscanthus sinensis
    M. s. 'Gracillimus' *88*
    M. s. 'Zebrinus' *88*
Miss Willmott's ghost *see Eryngium giganteum*
mock orange *see Philadelphus coronarius* 'Variegatus'
moneywort *see Lysimachia nummularia*
monkey flower *see Mimulus × burnetii*
monkshood *see Aconitum* 'Bressingham Spire'
Moroccan broom *see Cytisus battandieri*
Morus nigra 63
mountain avens *see Dryas octopetala*
mountain dogwood *see Cornus nuttallii*
mourning widow *see Geranium phaeum*
mullein *see Verbascum chaixii*
musk *see Mimulus × burnetii*
Myosotis
    M. scorpioides 76, 91
      M. s. 'Mermaid' 76
    M. sylvestris 51
Myriophyllum
    M. aquaticum 91
    M. verticillatum 91
myrtle flag *see Acorus calamus*
Myrtus communis 23, 67

nasturtium *see Tropaeolum*
Nepeta
    N. 'Six Hills Giant' *20*, 23
    N. × faassenii 20, 67, 79
Nerine 23
New Zealand flax *see Phormium tenax*
New Zealand laburnum *see Sophora tetraptera*
Nigella damascena 63
    N. d. 'Miss Jekyll' *63*
    N. d. 'Persian Jewells' *63*
northern maidenhair fern *see Adiantum pedatum*
Norway maple *see Acer platanoides*
Nuphar lutea 88
Nymphaea
    N. alba 88
    N. 'James Brydon' *89*
    N. × helvola 88
Nymphoides peltata 89

Oenothera missouriensis 21
Olearia × haastii 23
Ontario poplar *see Populus × candicans*
Oregon grape *see Mahonia aquifolium*
Oriental bittersweet *see Celastrus orbiculatus*
Oriental poppy *see Papaver orientale*
ornamental sea kale *see Crambe cordifolia*
ornamental rhubarb *see Rheum palmatum*
Orontium aquaticum 91
Osmanthus 35, 51, 67, 91
    O. delavayi 63
    O. heterophyllus 63

Osmunda 9
    O. regalis 89
      Cristata Group *89*
    O. regalis purpurascens 89
Osteospermum 23
    O. 'Buttermilk' *21*
    O. 'Cannington Roy' *21*
    O. 'Silver Sparkler' *21*
    O. 'Tresco Purple' *21*
    O. 'Whirligig' *21*
ostrich feather fern *see Matteuccia struthiopteris*
Ostrya
    O. carpinifolia 63
    O. virgiana 63
Ourisia macrophylla 48
Oxalis acetosella 35
Oxydendrum arboreum 48

Pachysandra terminalis 35
Pacific dogwood *see Cornus nuttallii*
Paeonia
    P. delavayi 64
    P. lactiflora Hybrids *33*
      P. l. 'White Wings' *33*
      P. l. 'Witleyi Major' *33*
    P. mlokosewitschii 33
pampas grass *see Cortaderia selloana*
Papaver orientale
    P. o. 'Black and White' *21*
    P. o. 'Mrs Perry' *21*
Parrotia 9
    P. persica 21, 91
      P. p. 'Pendula' *21*
parrot's feather *see Myriophyllum aquaticum*
Parthenocissus 9, 35
    P. tricuspidata 23

peach-leaved bellflower *see Campanula persicifolia*
pearl bush *see Exochorda × macrantha* 'The Bride'
pencil cedar *see Juniperus virgiana*
Penstemon 67, 79
    P. 'Alice Hindley' 211
    P. 'Andenken an Friedrich Hahn' *21*
    P. 'Apple Blossom' *21*
peony *see Paeonia*
perennial larkspur *see Delphinium* 'Lord Butler'
Perovskia
    P. atriplicifolia 21, 67
    P. a. 'Blue Spire' *21*
Persian candytuft *see Aethionema* 'Warley Ruber'
Persian ironwood *see Parrotia persica*
Persicaria bistorta 70, *71*, 91
    P. b. 'Superba' *77*
Philadelphus 23, 67, 71, 79
    P. coronarius
      P. c. 'Aureus' *64*
      P. c. 'Variegatus' *64*
Phillyrea latifolia 64
Phlomis fruticosa 23, 51, *64*
Phlox paniculata 23, 67
    P. p. 'Amethyst' *77*
    P. p. 'Franz Schubert' *77*
    P. p. 'Fujiyama' *77*
    P. p. 'Norah Leigh' *77*

Phormium
    P. 'Dazzler' 77
    P. tenax 23, 77
Phygelius capensis 23
Phyllostachys viridiglaucescens 33
Picea pungens 'Koster' 48
pickerel weed *see Pontederia cordata*
Pieris 9
    P. 'Forest Flame' 48
    P. japonica
        P. j. 'Firecrest' 48
        P. j. 'Variegata' 48
pin oak *see Quercus palustris*
pineapple broom *see Cytisus battandieri*
pink *see Dianthus* 'Doris'
pitcher plant *see Darlingtonia californica*
plantain lily *see Hosta fortunei*
plume poppy *see Macleaya microcarpa*
Polygonatum × *hybridum 33*, 51, 67, 79
Polypodium vulgare 35, 91
Polystichum setiferum 27, *89*
Pontederia cordata 89
Populus 91
    P. alba 23
        P. a. 'Raket' *64*
        P. a. 'Richardii' *64*
    P. × *canadensis*
        P. × *c.* 'Aurea' *89*
        P. × *c.* 'Serotina' *89*
    P. × *candicans* 'Aurora' 77
Potamogeton crispus 91
Potentilla fruticosa 23
    P. f. 'Abbotswood' *64*
    P. f. 'Hopley's Orange' *64*
    P. f. 'Red Ace' *64*
prickly rhubarb *see Gunnera manicata*
prickly thrift *see Acantholimon glumaceum*
pride of India *see Koelreuteria paniculata*
Primula 51
    P. auricula 'Adrian' 67
    P. florindae 79, *90*
    P. pulverulenta 90
        Bartley Hybrids *90*
        P. p. 'Bartley Pink' *90*
    P. vialii 83
Prunus 9
    P. laurocerasus 35
    P. padus 91
    P. sargentii 65
Pseudolarix amabilis 48
Pseudotsuga menziesii 49
    P.m. var. *glauca 49*
Pterocarya fraxinifolia 77, 91
Pulmonaria saccharata 35, 67, 79
pussy willow *see Salix caprea*
Pyracantha 9, 35
    P. 'Orange Glow' 77
Pyrus 67, 79
    P. calleryana 78
    P. 'Chanticleer' 78

Quercus palustris 78

rabbit's ears *see Stachys byzantina*
ragged robin *see Lychnis flos-cuculi*
Ranunculus
    R. acris 'Flore Pleno' *81, 90*
    R. aquatilis 90
red buckeye *see Aesculus pavia*
red maple *see Acer rubrum*
red valerian *see Centranthus ruber*
red-barked dogwood *see Cornus alba*
red-berried elder *see Sambucus racemosa*
red-hot poker *see Kniphofia* 'Royal
    Standard'
redbud tree *see Cercis siliquastrum*
reed mace *see Typha latifolia*
Rheum palmatum 78, *90*, 91
Rhododendron 35, 51
    R. davidsonianum 49
    R. 'Kirin' *49*
Rhodohypoxis baurii 49
rhubarb *see Rheum palmatum*
Rhus
    R. hirta 23
    R. typhina 23
Ribes laurifolium 67

rice paper plant *see Fatsia japonica*
Robinia 54
    R. hispida 65
    R. pseudoacacia 35
rock rose *see Cistus* × *cyprius*;
    Helianthemum 'Amy Baring'
Rodgersia pinnata 91
    R. p. 'Superba' *78*
Romneya coulteri 23, *65*
Rosa
    R. 'Königin von Dänemark' 35, *67*
    R. 'Madame Legras de Saint
        Germain' 35, *67*
    R. 'Maigold' 35
    R. 'Roseraie de Laÿ' *55*
    R. rugosa 9
rose acacia *see Robinia hispida*
rosemary *see Rosmarinus officinalis*
Rosmarinus 9
    R. officinalis 23, *65*, 67
royal fern *see Osmunda regalis*
rue *see Ruta graveolens*
Russian sage *see Perovskia atriplicifolia*
Ruta graveolens
    R. g. 'Jackman's Blue' *22*
    R. g. 'Variegata' *22*

sage *see Salvia officinalis* Purpurascens
    Group
Sagittaria sagittifolia 90
    S. s. 'Flore Pleno' 90
St Dabeoc's heath *see Daboecia cantabrica*
St John's wort *see Hypericum*
Salix 35, 91
    S. babylonica var. *pekinensis*
        'Tortuosa' *78*
    S. caprea 78
Salvia officinalis 9, 67, 79
    Purpurascens Group *22*
    S. o. 'Icterina' *22*
Sambucus 23, 51, 91
    S. racemosa 65, *79*
        S. r. 'Plumosa Aurea' *65*
Santolina chamaecyparissus 23, 51, 67, 79
Saponaria ocymoides 23, *53*
Sarcococca
    S. hookeriana 67, 79, 91
sargent cherry *see Prunus sargentii*
Scabiosa 9
    S. 'Butterfly Blue' *65*
    S. caucasica 'Clive Greaves' *65*
    S. 'Miss Willmott' *65*
    S. 'Pink Mist' *65*
scarlet trumpet honeysuckle *see Lonicera* ×
    brownii
Schizophragma
    S. hydrangeoides 33, 35
    S. integrifolium 33
Scotch heather *see Calluna vulgaris*
sea holly *see Eryngium bourgatii*
Senecio 'Sunshine' 12, 19, *22*, 67
shallon *see Gaultheria shallon*
shasta daisy *see Leucanthemum* × *superbum*
shooting star *see Dodecatheon pulchellum*
showy lady's slipper orchid *see*
    Cypripedium reginae
shrubby germander *see Teucrium fruticans*
shuttlecock fern *see Matteuccia struthiopteris*
Siberian bugloss *see Brunnera macrophylla*
silver bell tree *see Halesia monticola*
Sisyrinchium striatum 23
Skimmia japonica 34, 91
    S. j. 'Rubella' *34*
Smilacina racemosa 34
snakeweed *see Persicaria bistorta*
snowberry *see Symphoricarpos* × *doorenbosii*
    'Mother of Pearl'
snowdrop tree *see Halesia monticola*
snowy mespilus *see Amelanchier canadensis*
soft shield fern *see Polystichum setiferum*
Solomon's seal *see Polygonatum* × *hybridum*
Sophora
    S. microphylla 'Early Gold' *22*
    S. tetraptera 22
Sorbaria aitchisonii 79
Sorbus 51, 67
    S. aucuparia 35

sorrel tree *see Oxydendrum arboreum*
Spanish broom *see Spartium junceum*
Spartium junceum 22
spiderwort *see Tradescantia* × *andersoniana*
    'Purple Dome'
Spiraea 23
    S. betulifolia 66
    S. japonica 'Goldflame' 66
Stachys 9
    S. byzantina 22
        S. b. 'Silver Carpet' 22
Stachyurus chinensis 66
staff vine *see Celastrus orbiculatus*
Staphylea
    S. colchica 49
    S. holocarpa 'Rosea' *49*
star magnolia *see Magnolia stellata*
Stepanandra tanakae 67, 79
Stewartia 9
    S. pseudocamellia 34
        Koreana Group 34
    S. sinensis 34, *49*
Stipa gigantea 23
storax *see Styrax officinalis*
Stratiotes aloides 91
Styrax officinalis 50
summer hyacinth *see Galtonia candicans*
sun rose *see Helianthemum* 'Amy Baring'
swamp cypress *see Taxodium distichum*
sweet flag *see Acorus calamus*
sweet gum *see Liquidambar styraciflua*
sweet violet *see Viola riviniana*
Symphoricarpos
    S. × *doorenbosii* 23, 35, 91
        S. × *d.* 'Mother of Pearl' 66
    S. orbiculatus 66
Symphytum
    S. grandiflorum 34
    S. 'Hidcote Blue' 34
    S. × *uplandicum* 'Variegatum' *34*
Syringa 51, 67, 79
    S. × *henryi* 66

tamarisk *see Tamarix ramosissima*
Tamarix ramosissima 23
    T. r. 'Rosea' 23
    T. r. 'Rubra' 23
Tarpa natans 91
Taxodium distichum 50, 79, 91
Taxus 9
Tellima grandiflora 34
Teucrium fruticans 23, 66
Thalictrum aquilegiifolium var. *album 34*
Thuja
    T. occidentalis 'Sunkist' 66
    T. plicata 'Zebrina' 66
Thymus herba-barona 23
torch lily *see Kniphofia* 'Royal Standard'
Tradescantia 35, 51, 79
    T. × *andersoniana*
        T. × *a.* 'Blue Stone' 79
        T. × *a.* 'Purple Dome' *79*
tree mallow *see Lavatera* 'Barnsley'
tree peony *see Paeonia delavayi*
Trillium grandiflorum 35, 50, 91
trinity flower *see Trillium grandiflorum*
Trollius
    T. europaeus 35, 79
    T. × *cultorum*
        T. × *c.* 'Canary Bird' 35
        T. × *c.* 'Orange Princess' 35

Tropaeolum 27
    T. speciosum 35, *50*
trumpet flower *see Campsis radicans*
trumpet vine *see Campsis radicans*
Tsuga heterophylla 50, 91
tumbling Ted *see Saponaria ocymoides*
Typha latifolia 91

umbrella grass *see Cyperus involucratus*
umbrella plant *see Darmera peltata*
Uvularia grandiflora 50

Vaccinium
    V. corymbosum 51
    V. glaucoalbum 51
Veratrum
    V. album 35
    V. nigrum 35
Verbascum
    V. chaixii 67
    V. nigrum 23
Veronica prostrata 23, 51, 67, 79
Viburnum 9, 51, 67, 79
    V. opulus 79
        V. o. 'Aureum' 79
        V. o. 'Xanthocarpus' 79
    V. plicatum 'Mariesii' *51*
    V. pulverulenta 91
    V. tinus 67
Vinca 67
    V. minor 79
        V. m. 'Argenteovariegata' *51*
Viola 23, 51
    V. riviniana Purpurea Group 35
Virginian cowslip *see Mertensia*
    pulmonarioides
Vitis 9
    V. coignetiae 23
Voss's laburnum *see Laburnum* x *watereri*
    'Vossii'

wake robin *see Trillium grandiflorum*
wallflower *see Erysimum cheiri*
water chestnut *see Tarpa natans*
water crowfoot *see Ranunculus aquatilis*
water fern *see Azolla filiculoides*
water forget-me-not *see Myosotis*
    scorpioides
water fringe *see Nymphoides peltata*
water hawthorn *see Aponogeton distachyos*
water lily *see Nymphaea*
water milfoil *see Myriophyllum verticillatum*
water plantain *see Alisma plantago-aquatica*
water soldier *see Stratiotes aloides*
water violet *see Hottonia palustris*
Weigela florida 'Foliis Purpureis' 67
Welsh poppy *see Meconopsis cambrica*
western hemlock *see Tsuga heterophylla*
white poplar *see Populus alba* 'Raket'
whortleberry *see Vaccinium corymbosum*
willow gentian *see Gentiana asclepiadea*
Wisteria 9
witch hazel *see Hamamelis* x *intermedia*
wolfbane *see Aconitum* 'Bressingham
    Spire'
wood lily *see Trillium grandiflorum*
wood spurge *see Euphorbia amygdaloides*
    var. *robbiae*

yarrow *see Achillea filipendulina*
yellow flag *see Iris pseudacorus*
yellow lupin *see Lupinus luteus*
yellow skunk cabbage *see Lysichiton*
    americanus
yellow water lily *see Nuphar lutea*
Yucca filamentosa 23
    Y. f. 'Variegata' 23
    Y. f. 'Bright Edge' 23

Zantedeschia 83
Zauschneria
    Z. californica 23
    Z. c. ssp. *cana* 'Dublin' 23
zebra grass *see Miscanthus sinensis*
Zenobia 9
    Z. pulverulenta 51

EDITOR'S NOTE

Many people are confused by the rules of nomenclature and a brief explanation may help to clarify any confusion. All plants belong to **families**. This is a biological grouping and each family contains plants which have similar flowers, fruits and organs. Within each family there are recognizable groups of plants, for example geraniums (*geranium*) which belong to the family *Geraniaceae,* or roses (*rosa*) which belong to the family *Rosaceae.* Each group is known as a **genus**.

A genus contains one, or, more often, a number of **species**. For instance *Geranium pratense* is one species of the genus *geranium* and in reference books both words appear in italics with no capital letter for the species name.

Species can be sub-divided into three categories, although they don't have to be: **sub-species**, written ssp. which means it is a distinct variant of the species plant, probably because it comes from a different geographical location. *G. asphodeloides* ssp. *crenophilum* would be an example; **varieties** written var. which stands for *varietas.* This means the botanical structure is slightly different, for instance, *G. grandiflorum* var. *alpinum* (large-flowered Alpine variety); and **forms** written f. which stands for *forma.* This would generally mean a slight change, like different colouring of the leaf or flower, for example *G. pratense* f. *albiflorum* (the white-flowered form of the meadow cranesbill).

Plants have been grown and bred for generations and the majority of plants grown in gardens and listed in reference books are individual **cultivars** (cultivated varieties). Since 1959 these have been shown by a common name printed in roman type within quotation marks. This distinguishes this type of plant from varieties from the wild which are printed in italics. Cultivars may be derived from the species plant: *Geranium pratense* 'Mrs Kendall Clark', from the subspecies, *G. sessiliflorum* ssp. *novae-zelandiae* 'Porter's Pass'; and from the variant, *G. phaeum* var. *lividus* 'Majus'.

For practical purposes that only leaves **hybrids** which are sexual crosses between two, botanically distinct, species or genera. This is shown by the hybrid multiplication sign. An example of the latter is ✕ *Halimiocistus* which is a hybrid genus of *Cistus* ✕ *halimium*. More commonly a hybrid is a cross between one species within a genus and another, such as *Geranium* ✕ *oxonianum*. Very often, in these cases, cultivars of the hybrid are better known than the hybrid itself. A good example of this is *G.* ✕ *o.* 'Wargrave Pink'. Hybrids are extremely common and very often, where the parentage is difficult or unclear they are denoted by giving the cultivar name after the generic name, for instance, *Geranium* 'Ann Folkard'.

Name Changes

Many well known plants have changed their name recently and this is often a source of irritation to many gardeners. These changes are made to achieve greater accuracy in plant names. The Editorial Panel of *The Plant Finder* (published by Dorling Kindersley) lists at the back of that book a comprehensive list of reverse synonyms which will enable anyone to track down a plant whose name may have changed: *pernettya, arundinaria* and *chrysanthemum* are three obvious examples. The list is very large and a copy of *The Plant Finder* is a good investment for this alone, along with its other virtues.

ACKNOWLEDGEMENTS

The publishers would like to thank the following picture libraries and photographers for supplying the pictures used in this book. The pictures are numbered according to their position on the page and are identified by the page number first and position second. The position is numbered 1-6 reading from top left to bottom right on each page.

Sue Atkinson & Sue Atkinson Library
40/4-5, 41/1-5, 42/3-4-5, 43/ -4, 44//3, 45/2-4-6, 46/4, 47/1-2-6, 48/1-5, 50/2-3-4-5-6, 51/1-2-3, 56/1-2-3-4, 57/4-5-6,

58/1-4-5-6, 59/3-4, 60/1-2, 61/1-4-5-6, 62/3, 63/1-3-6, 64/1-2-3-4-6, 65/2-4-5-6, 66/1-4-6, 72/4-6, 73/3-4-5, 74/3-6, 75/1-4-5-6, 76/1-5, 77/1-3-4, 78/2-4, 79/2, 84/1-2, 85/2-6, 86/1-4, 87/5-6, 88/1-3-5, 89/3-4, 90/1-2-5, 91/3, 28/1-3-4, 29/1-2-4-5-6, 30/1-2-4-5, 31/2-3-4-5-6, 32/1-2-3-4-5, 33/2-5-6, 34/1-2, 34/4-6, 35/1-3 14/3-6, 15/2-5-6, 16/1-2-4-5-6, 17/ 3-4-5, 18/2-3-5, 19/4-6, 20/1-6, 21/1-6, 22/2-5, 23/1.

Gillian Beckett
42/2, 43/2, 44/4, 46/3, 47/5, 59/1, 62/4, 63/2, 65/3, 66/5, 67/2-3, 72/1, 28/2, 34/5, 22/3.

The Garden Picture Library
56/1, 60/2, 73/4, 20/5.

Bob Gibbons/Natural Image
45/3, 46/6, 63/4, 73/1, 74/5, 91/2, 19/1, 23/2.

John Glover
40/2, 41/3, 44/5, 45/1, 57/2, 59/6, 66/3, 74/4, 75/3, 20/4.

Brian Matthews
49/4, 60/4-5, 62/2, 66/2, 76/4, 77/5, 22/6.

Peter McHoy
40/6, 41/2-6, 42/1, 43/5-6, 44/1-2-6, 48/3-6, 49/1-6, 50/1, 56/6, 61/3, 62/5, 65/1, 73/2-6, 74/1-2, 75/2, 76/6, 77/6, 79/1-3, 84/3-6, 85/3-4, 88/6, 89/5, 90/4-6, 91/1, 28/5-6, 29/3, 31/1, 33/3, 34/3, 14/2-5, 15/3-4, 17/6, 18/1-4-6, 22/4.

Harry Smith Collection
40/1-3, 41/4, 42/6, 43/3, 45/5, 46/1-2-5, 47/3-4, 48/2-4, 49/2, 49/3, 56/5, 57/1-3, 58/2-3, 59/2-5, 60/3-6, 61/2, 62/1-6, 63/5, 64/5, 67/1, 72/2-3-5, 76/2-3, 77/2, 78/1-3-5-6, 84/4-5, 85/1-5, 86/2-3-5-6, 87/3-4, 88/2-1, 89/1-2-6, 90/3, 30/3-6, 32/6, 33/1-4, 35/2, 14/1-4, 16/3, 17/1-2, 19/2-3-5, 20/2-5, 21/2-3-5, 22/1, 23/3